DAVID FELLMAN
*Vilas Professor of Political Science*
*University of Wisconsin*
ADVISORY EDITOR TO DODD, MEAD & COMPANY

# POLITICS OF FEDERAL HOUSING

# Politics of Federal Housing

HAROLD WOLMAN

DODD, MEAD & COMPANY

*New York     1971     Toronto*

FOR MY PARENTS

# PREFACE

The purpose of this study is to describe and analyze the housing policy process involving redistributive outputs at the national level. Its organization follows generally the discussion of political systems in Chapter 1. Thus, Chapter 2 discusses the values in question (housing in America), while Chapter 3 deals with what portion of those values are allocated outside the public sector and delineates the environment of the housing political system. Chapters 4–7 describe the conversion process of each of four subsystems within the housing policy system. Chapter 8 deals with the characteristics and composition of the decision-making elite involved in the conversion process, and also analyzes and discusses the attitudes of this elite. As this brief outline indicates, the study focuses on the conversion process of the housing political system—that is, the actual decision-making process and the decision-making elite involved.

The study covers intensively the period from 1965–67, starting with the birth of HUD and ending nearly a year before the demise of the Johnson Administration. It covers much less intensively the period from 1967–69. Interviewing for the study took place during the fall and winter of 1967 and spring of 1968.

HAROLD WOLMAN

## Acknowledgments

I would like to express sincere gratitude to the Washington Center for Metropolitan Studies and its president, Professor Royce Hanson, for providing me with office facilities for the year in which I was in Washington conducting research. The staff of the Center—particularly Mrs. Carla Cohen, Mrs. Janice Lessel, James T. Hughes, David Parry, George Grier, Milan Dluhy, and Verrick O. French—provided me with invaluable assistance and advice.

I would also like to thank Professor Robert Wood, Undersecretary of the Department of Housing and Urban Development during the time in which the research was conducted, for the cooperation his office and his assistants—particularly Mr. John Zuccoti and Mr. Joseph Freitus—gave to me.

Professor Norman Thomas, Professor Robert Friedman, Professor Morton J. Schussheim, Mr. Douglas Ross, Mr. Ben Laime, Mr. Joseph Ball, and Mr. David Cohen all provided needed advice and criticism. A debt of gratitude is also due to Miss Ann Brueckmann, Miss Anne Carney, and Mrs. Soila Houser for their editorial assistance. Finally, but most importantly, I wish to thank my wife Dianne for her aid and encouragement.

# CONTENTS

## *Tables*

# POLITICS OF FEDERAL HOUSING

# CHAPTER 1

# Politics and Public Policy

## Politics

Politics is the process by which values are authoritatively allocated in a society.[1] Disputed values are those things desired by an individual or group of individuals which if satisfied would conflict with what is desired by other individuals or groups of individuals. Conflict in this context exists either because the disputed values are at least to some extent mutually exclusive (e.g., there should be a state church vs. there should not be a state church) or because the values are scarce (resources should be put to use to aid poor people in cities rather than farmers).

All allocation of disputed values, however, is not accomplished through the process of politics. Rather politics is the authoritative allocation of values; it is *one* of the processes by which values are distributed in a society. In general terms, "authoritative" here implies that the final decision is made in the public sector, even though there may have been wide participation in the decision by nonpublic groups. In fact, many important conflicts over disputed values are resolved wholly through private societal institutions such as the family, the church, the corporation, or a variety of others. Disputed values enter the realm of politics only when conflict becomes, in E. E. Schattschneider's term, "socialized"—that is,

[1] David Easton, *The Political System* (New York: Alfred A. Knopf, 1953), Chap. 5.

moved into the public arena.[2] Obviously, disputed values which are allocated nonpolitically are not unimportant; indeed, in many cases, they may be of primary importance.[3]

## The Political System

"Political system" may be defined as the system of human inter-actions in any society through which disputed values are authorita-tively allocated.[4] A political system, therefore, is an analytical con-struct, an abstraction from reality; it does not attempt to explain relationships between variables, but rather provides a framework for doing so. A subsystem is an analytically consistent component of a larger system (thus, state politics can be looked at as a subsys-tem of American politics or zoning can be viewed as a subsystem of municipal politics).

All political systems (indeed, all systems) consist of the same components. The environment defines the problem for the political system and sets limits on possible responses. Inputs enter the polit-ical system (or a particular subsystem) from the environment in the form of demands (disputed values). These demands are then

---

[2] E. E. Schattschneider, *The Semi-Sovereign People* (New York: Holt, Rine-hart and Winston, 1960), p. 39. Schattschneider attempts, in this thought-pro-voking book, to explain why disputes move from the private to the public level.

[3] This distinction forms the nucleus of a bitter debate between political sci-entists and sociologists concerning the nature of community power structures. Sociologists accuse political scientists of studying only decisions made in the public arena, whereas political scientists accuse sociologists of ignoring gov-ernment decisions. See particularly the exchange of letters between Thomas Anton and Robert A. Dahl, *Administrative Science Quarterly*, VIII (Septem-ber, 1963). Herbert Kaufmann has suggested that the disputed values (stakes) which are most often allocated by the political system are: the winning of elective or appointive office, distribution of government services, distribution of public costs (taxing and borrowing), public regulation of economic activity, and enforcement of standards. Herbert Kaufmann, *Politics and Policies in State and Local Governments* (Englewood Cliffs, N.J.: Prentice-Hall, 1963), pp. 66–74.

[4] David Easton, *A Framework for Political Analysis* (Englewood Cliffs, N.J.: Prentice-Hall, 1965), p. 50.

"converted"—in David Easton's terms [5]—into outputs by the inter-actions which take place inside the system. The outputs (in the form of policies) flow into the environment, but they also reenter the system once again as feedback through additional demands and support which the policies and their impact have generated.

A system may, of course, be considered analytically as distinct from its environment (indeed this is what must be done or every study would be a study of the universe). In this case, the environ-ment is viewed as a set of constraints or limits upon the system. By the same token, it must be realized that any system is itself com-posed of numerous subsystems and that the internal processes of a particular system in turn comprise inputs and outputs for the var-ious subsystems.

The environment of any system is, of course, not undifferen-tiated: only certain demands enter the system and only some of these are important in determining output. Those groups or indi-viduals who have access to points of decision-making within the system are more likely to receive system outputs which meet with their favor than those who lack such access. As this suggests, the basic unit of analysis for the processes within the system itself is the decision. Outputs (or policies) consist of sets of decisions.

It is immediately apparent that except in a utopia where each person has equal influence, the importance of participants within the system in determining outputs will vary. Some will be more "powerful" than others. Power is a concept which political phi-losophers—and more recently political scientists—have strug-gled with for centuries in an effort to arrive at a clear and agreed upon definition. To this point, the only agreement reached is that it is nearly impossible to discuss politics without reference to the elusive concept of power. Each political scientist must still specify exactly what it is that *he* means by the term "power." As used here, power is conceptualized as a relationship between or among indi-viduals who are attempting to produce a policy output. Thus, an

---

[5] *Ibid.*, p. 131.

individual is powerful if he has an effect on that series of decisions (or "nondecisions") concerned with important policy changes and if that effect is consistent with his intentions.[6] The reasons for his influence (the term "influence" shall be used synonymously with "power") may vary with the individual. Possible reasons (resource bases) for power include money, respect, expertise, position, control of a voting bloc, as well as various others. Those individuals who are the most powerful are termed the "elite." The existence of a decision-making elite in a political system is thus *not* an empirical question; it is postulated by definition.[7] Empirical research may focus on the *nature* of that elite, but not on its existence.

What are the questions one would be most interested in asking about a political system in general? The first would undoubtedly concern the disputed values (inputs) which are allocated through the system. What are they and what is their nature? How many disputed values of importance and, indeed, what sorts of them are allocated through other systems? What are the disputed values which are allocated specifically through the political system? Other questions of critical importance concerning input might be these: What are the environmental constraints on the political system which limit and define its operations, including ideological constraints? Who has access to the system's decision-making elite and who does not?

In the conversion process itself, what are the processes through which disputed values are allocated? What are the characteristics and composition of the decision-making elite which allocate them —or in Robert A. Dahl's terms, who governs?[8] To what degree are

---

[6] The effect may be any one of several different kinds. It may be concerned with a decision on general priorities (should we push housing or education or neither), decisions on substance (what should be the exact nature of the program), decisions on political strategy, or decisions concerned with needed approval or disapproval (persuading Congressmen to support or oppose a proposal).

[7] Harold Lasswell and Abraham Kaplan, *Power and Society* (New Haven, Conn.: Yale University Press, 1950), pp. 55–56.

[8] Robert A. Dahl, *Who Governs?* (New Haven: Yale University Press, 1961).

the various interests and values in dispute represented within this elite? How representative is this elite of society in general? How do individuals enter the elite? How open is the elite to influence from the outside?

On the output side, who gets what? What is the impact of these allocative decisions? Finally, in terms of feedback, what new demands are generated by the way disputed values are allocated in previous decisions?

## The Structure of Power Within the Political System

The tradition within the discipline of political science in this country (although there are significant exceptions) is to describe the American political system as a pluralist democracy. This analysis of the political system has been closely associated with "group theory" and the group approach to politics, the group being a concept which has fascinated political scientists ever since Arthur Bentley declared: "The great task in the study of any form of social life is the analysis of these groups. . . . When the groups are adequately stated, everything is stated. When I say everything, I mean everything." [9]

Bentley, of course, was not saying here, as writers less sophisticated than he have suggested, that policy outputs are determined solely by the interplay of pressure groups. Rather, when Bentley said "group" he meant "interest," [10] or in David Truman's words "shared attitudes." [11] Thus Bentley recognized two different types of groups, organized groups and discussion groups—the latter roughly corresponding to what Truman calls "potential groups." According to Truman, people with any mutual interest, or with shared attitudes or expectations, are potential groups. He goes on

---

[9] Arthur F. Bentley, *The Process of Government* (Bloomington, Ind.: Principia Press, 1908), p. 208. In Bentley's terms, the group approach was not evaluative, but was a way of organizing information.

[10] *Ibid.*, p. 211.

[11] David Truman, *The Governmental Process* (New York: Alfred A. Knopf, 1951), p. 34.

to note that "only a portion of the interests or attitudes involved in such expectations are represented by organized groups."[12] Public policy outputs then are viewed as the resultant equilibrium of the various forces (groups) involved. The institutions of government are viewed as the arena of group conflict and as extensions of it,[13] with political parties considered one of the most important transmission belts by which these groups reach the governmental area.

Thus groups strive to gain control of key points of decision within the government.[14] If control is not possible, they attempt to achieve effective access to those key points so that they will influence those who do hold them (those who have previously been termed the "decision-making elite"). As Truman notes: "Towards whatever institution of government we observe interest groups operating, the common feature of all their efforts is the attempt to achieve effective access to points of decision."[15]

All groups, of course, do not automatically receive effective access (influence) to the decision-making elite. Influence may occur because members of the elite personally share the views of groups (either organized or potential) or because a group convinces members of the elite that it is to the latter's advantage to grant effective access. This second manner of gaining influence is almost always open only to organized groups.

Speaking in terms of the group model, Dahl concludes that the American political system is a pluralist democracy. He describes the "normal" American political process as one in which "there is a

[12] *Ibid.*, p. 511.

[13] This has led, in some instances, to an underemphasis on the positive role public officials themselves may play in determining policy outputs. Thus, William Mitchell contends, "the model seems to attribute most of the initiative to groups and very little to the officials. But while the criticism is probably more true of Bentley's work than of Truman's, even the latter's image of the political system is one that makes the government something worked upon. As a result, the possible influence of the tighter system of bureaucratic norms working on officialdom . . . has not been given much attention." William C. Mitchell, *The American Polity* (Glencoe, Ill.: The Free Press, 1962), pp. 84–85.

[14] A classic example is the railroad industry's control over the I.C.C.

[15] Truman, *op. cit.* (n. 11), p. 264.

high probability that an active and legitimate group in the population can make itself heard effectively at some crucial stage in the process of decision." [16] Decisions are made through endless bargaining between these various groups. Thus Dahl specifies the manner through which, in the group model, contending groups arrive at a balance of forces—namely bargaining, a process which implies trading off, compromise, some degree of mutuality of interest. No one group dominates the decision-making process.

Since the mid-1950's, a number of social scientists led by C. Wright Mills and Floyd Hunter have questioned whether the American political system can really be described as a pluralist democracy. They have contended with some vigor that the political system is in fact elitist. According to this view, people with certain sets of shared attitudes are likely to lack the necessary resource bases to give them effective access. One of the most important of these resource bases is organization per se. Obviously there are some potential groups which, despite their relevance, have been unable to organize effectively. This means that interests of large numbers of people remain unarticulated and unrepresented in the making of decisions unless those interests are held by others who do have influence. Thus, through this form of virtual representation, middle-class white liberals for years brought some of the interests of poor Negroes into the decision-making process.

Particularly, as Robert Lane points out, lower class people with little education and low political efficacy are less likely to join groups than are their middle and upper class counterparts.[17] In some cases, there may be actual legal or social prohibitions against members of the lower class forming certain types of groups. All this leads Robert Presthus to comment:

Pluralists maintain that bargaining among . . . organizations culminates roughly in the "public interest." However, this rationale has one rather pressing shortcoming, namely that all interests are not equally repre-

[16] Robert A. Dahl, A Preface to Democratic Theory (Chicago: University of Chicago Press, 1956), p. 145.
[17] Robert E. Lane, Political Life (New York: The Free Press, 1959), p. 16.

sented in the bargaining arena. Real competition on any specific issue is limited to relatively few powerful groups. . . . These structural facets of contemporary pluralism mean that bargaining often proceeds among a presidium which disadvantages unorganized segments of society.[18]

The criticism of the pluralists has led to a debate of fierce proportions swirling around the question of whether the political system is in fact pluralist or elitist. Much of the research on the subject has been conducted at the community level; I shall forego any comprehensive discussion of this literature because it has already been competently discussed and dissected elsewhere.[19]

What can be concluded from this literature is that there is little general agreement on what is meant by pluralism and elitism. Indeed, it may be that these ambiguous concepts do not provide very useful categories for classifying power structures of political systems or subsystems. Theodore Lowi and Robert Salisbury have each separately attacked analyses which have characterized entire political systems in this manner. The pluralists sometimes suggest, for example, that if all subsystems are characterized by the same power structure, then and only then is the system elitist; otherwise it is pluralist. Lowi contends that this is a meaningless approach, and that it may be impossible to classify an entire political system as either pluralist or elitist. Rather, he suggests there may be several different types of decisional categories in a political system and the power structure may vary with the types. Lowi calls these types "arenas of power" and identifies three: distributive, regulative, and redistributive.[20] These three decisional categories, although perhaps not a complete list of identifiable arenas of power,

[18] Robert Presthus, *Men at the Top* (New York: Oxford University Press, 1964), p. 31.

[19] For a comprehensive (though somewhat biased towards the pluralist viewpoint) review of the literature, see Nelson W. Polsby, *Community Power and Political Theory* (New Haven, Conn.: Yale University Press, 1963). See also John Walton, "The Current State of Research on Community Power," *American Journal of Sociology* (January, 1966).

[20] Theodore J. Lowi, "Distribution, Regulation, Redistribution; The Function of Government," *Public Policies and Their Politics*, ed. Randall B. Ripley (New York: W.W. Norton, 1966), p. 27.

nonetheless provide a very useful framework for the analysis of public policy. Differences between the three seem apparent:

1. Distributive decisions (such as tariff legislation, public works legislation, and most reconsiderations of major social programs such as housing, social security, and education). These are the decisions which Lowi claims the pluralists have studied to the exclusion of most others. They involve output which can be disaggregated so that there is *perceived* to be "something for everybody." The beneficiaries are perceived to be specific organized interests rather than broad classes of people. The output itself likely involves only an incremental change from that which preceded it.

2. Regulatory decisions (such as the Meat Inspection Act of 1967). These are decisions which are perceived to limit the freedom of action of an industry or institution (e.g., the stock market). In implementation these may involve decisions aimed at a specific organization, such as the antitrust suit against Standard Oil or the forced withdrawal of thalidomide by the Food and Drug Administration.

3. Redistributive decisions, which may involve social and economic values (as in the original passage of the poverty program). These are decisions which are *perceived* to involve aid to a large class of individuals. Indeed, in some cases they may involve class conflict in the Marxian sense. All redistributive decisions are not of this type, however—thus the 1965 Education Act redistributed values in favor of a religious class—Catholics.

The criterion used in selecting decisions for each arena, as Robert Salisbury points out, is the likely impact on society perceived by the decision-makers.[21]

Within each of these types of decisions there may be various processes by which outputs are arrived at. Thus, redistributive decisions can be made by any of a number of processes. In redistri-

[21] Robert Salisbury, "The Analysis of Public Policy: A Search for Theories and Roles," unpublished manuscript, p. 8.

butive housing decisions, for example, the most obvious process is Congressional passage of a modified Administration proposal (such as rent supplements); but there are clearly several other possibilities, such as the judicial process (restrictive convenant unconstitutional), Presidential order (Executive Order on nondiscrimination in housing), setting of administrative criteria ("urban renewal programs should be redirected so that they help the low-income Negro"). Each of these processes for each decision arena may have a different type of power structure and ought to be investigated independently so that generalizations can be drawn inductively.

What is it, then, about the power structure that ought to be studied if the simple dichotomy of pluralism-elitism offers no guide? Quite obviously the variables one might be interested in reflect the theoretical interests of the researcher. To the extent that social scientists agree on what interests them and thus agree on what variables to investigate, research of a comparative nature would be greatly facilitated. However, the mindless usage of the terms "pluralism" and "elitism" has blurred over the differences which do exist in theoretical interests, so that, much too often, social scientists are studying vastly different things but calling them by the same name.

Agger, Goldrich, and Swanson avoid this trap by developing a typology of power structures dependent upon the ideology of the

|  | Distribution of political power among citizens | |
|---|---|---|
| Political leaderships ideology | Broad | Narrow |
| Convergent | Consensual mass (consensus) | Consensual elite (power elite) |
| Divergent | Competitive mass (mass democracy) | Competitive elite (pluralist democracy) [22] |

[22] Robert G. Agger, Daniel Goldrich, and Burt Swanson, *The Rulers and the Ruled* (New York: John Wiley, 1964), p. 75.

political leadership (convergent or divergent) and the degree of distribution of political power among citizens (broad or narrow). In this scheme, four different types of power structure are possible.

A slight variant in the Agger, Goldrich, and Swanson effort provides an operationally more workable typology for classification of power structures. Instead of using the distribution of political power among citizens as one variable, the degree of access of groups (in the Bentley sense) to the decision-making elite is more meaningful since politics is primarily group rather than individual activity. Thus the typology would be:

*Degree of access of groups*
*to decision-making elite*

| *Political leaderships ideology* | Open | Closed |
|---|---|---|
| Convergent | Consensual (consensus) | Consensual elite (power elite) |
| Divergent | Competitive (representative democracy) | Competitive elite (pluralist democracy) [23] |

A description of the American political system would be comprised of a checkmark in one of the four categories of the typology for each decision process in each decision-making arena. The number of these processes, however, for some arenas may be very large. Therefore, in order to make the problem manageable (and to suggest divisions of labor), it is useful to add another dimension to the investigation. Although there is an element of subjectivity involved, policy outputs can be divided into categories of varying significance so far as impact on the society is concerned. Thus, some of the processes may be deemed to yield trivial outputs so far

[23] Within each of these quadrants other variables may be investigated. Thus, dominant resource bases or elite recruitment patterns (or various others) variables might be studied for each of the four types of political system.

as the society is concerned, while other outputs may result in (or prevent) significant social change. It is in these latter decisions that theorists are likely to be most interested, in their efforts to make a comprehensive evaluation of the political system.

## Object of Study

The object of the present study is to describe and analyze one example of a redistributive political system. The basic questions to be asked about this system are set forth on pp. 4–5. Political scientists have much too often ignored redistributive decisions and have concentrated instead mostly on distributive systems, which are admittedly more numerous and commonplace. However, insofar as the political system affects significant social change (a phenomenon which empirical political scientists have not studied extensively in this country), it is the redistributive system which bears studying.

The particular political system chosen was the one in which housing policy and more specifically, housing policy for low-income people, is determined.[24] Redistributive housing decisions (decisions whose impact is perceived by those involved in the decision-making process to favor a class of people) do not occur frequently. When they do, they are seen to be major changes, such as the Urban Renewal legislation of 1949 or the rent supplement legislation of 1965, both of which were programs perceived, at the time, as attempts to aid the lower class. The output of a redistributive decision, thus, is likely to be qualitatively different from what has preceded it; it is not likely to be an incremental change. Rather, it is likely to be perceived as significant social change. Most housing bills, indeed, are incremental-distributive rather than redistributive. They are mostly variations on a main theme (40,000 or 50,000 units of public housing, lowering the required

[24] Since all housing decisions clearly are not redistributive (indeed, only a few of them are), some light is also thrown by this investigation on a distributive political system.

downpayment on FHA housing, etc.), rather than a change in the theme itself or the addition of a new one.

Quite obviously, a study of one redistributive system cannot speak for all, nor does it intend to. It is, rather, a start which hopefully will serve as a comparative basis for similar studies of other redistributive systems. Despite the fact that only one political system is under consideration, this work does not intend to be, nor is it, what is traditionally known as a "case study." A case study is an intensive study of the process by which a specific decision or policy is arrived at. The present study, however, analyzes certain *types* of decisions and nondecisions (redistributive housing) and the decision-making elite which makes them.[25]

Housing was selected for study because it involves an allocation of quite important values which, particularly in terms of housing for low-income Americans, has only recently entered into the political sphere. The way in which the political system handles disputes which portend either significant social change or its prevention or modification (housing, employment, education, etc.) will bear great consequences for the entire social system. Political science, if it is to remain relevant, must move towards studying the political processes of change.

[25] For a detailed discussion of the methodology, see Appendix 1.

# CHAPTER 2

# The Values in Question— Housing in America

## The Housing Problem

Early housing reformers perceived "the housing problem" in relatively simple and unsophisticated terms. One group of reformers consisted of architects or quasi-architects who were impressed primarily with the visual ugliness and disorderliness of the slums. This aesthetic distaste for slums has become a progressively less important force in housing reform, although it has not by any means disappeared. A greater concern for social problems of human beings rather than problems of architectual aesthetics has both diminished the relative importance of architects and engineers as housing reformers and has instilled some degree of social concern into those who remain.

A second group equated slums with structurally poor housing and assumed that the latter was responsible for all the socially pathological behavior associated with the former. Roy Lubove, in discussing the Progressives' attitude towards this relationship, comments:

. . . the housing reformer had also considered better housing as an instrument of social control. He observed that tenement neighborhoods, populated often by foreigners and their children, seemed to abound in vice, crime, and pauperism. He assumed, therefore, that the physical en-

14

vironment was at fault. The tenement must cause a deterioration of character making the individual more susceptible to vice than he would have been in a different environment. Improve his housing, it followed, and you would influence his character for the better.[1]

During the 1930's when the federal government first began to address itself to the problems of slum and housing, the overriding importance of housing as the independent variable causing social disorganization was "established" in a number of studies carried out by the reformers.[2] The effect—indeed the design—of these studies was to buttress the reformers' case for public housing as a means of relocating slum dwellers from their destructive environment (substandard housing).

This view, however, has been under a steady two-sided attack since the 1940's. One attacking side has concentrated on the supposed social benefits associated with rehousing. Sociologists—such as Herbert Gans, Marc Fried, and Lee Rainwater—pointed out that there were positive values associated by inhabitants with even the most substandard dwellings. In basic terms, to most families, the dwelling unit was not simply a substandard structure, but a home infused with the life style of the family inhabiting it. Alvin Schorr reports the comments of a Milwaukee woman responding to a proposal to tear down houses in a "slum" where she lived: "Slums, they call us. Why that's a terrible word—those are our homes, our shrines. We live there." [3]

Lee Rainwater argues that the house, particularly for the lower class, ought to be viewed as a haven from the fear which permeates the individual in the outside world. He observes:

There is in our culture a long history of the development of the house as a place of safety from both nonhuman and human threats, a history

[1] Roy Lubove, "The Progressives and the Slums," *Urban Renewal: People, Politics and Planning*, ed. Jewell Bellush and Murray Hausknecht (New York: Anchor Books, 1967), p. 19.
[2] John Dean, "The Myths of Housing Reform," *ibid.*, p. 28.
[3] Alvin Schorr, *Slums and Social Insecurity*, U.S. Department of Health, Education, and Welfare, Research Report No. 1 (Washington: U.S. Government Printing Office, 1963), p. 9.

which culminates in guaranteeing the house, a man's castle, against unreasonable search and seizure. The house becomes the place of maximum exercise of individual autonomy, minimal conformity to the formal and complex rules of public demeanor. The house acquires a sacred character from its complex intertwining with the self and from the symbolic character it has as a representation of the family. These conceptions of the house are readily generalized to the area around it, to the neighborhood.[4]

As a result, although most people in poor housing undoubtedly wish to improve their situation, abandoning an old home is likely to involve some degree of psychological stress. Further, tearing down houses and neighborhoods and moving people into institutionalized public housing may have a lasting undesirable impact on some low-income people, for it may destroy the context of their social and familial life without replacing it with anything viable. As Marc Fried concludes:

Grieving for a lost home is evidently a widespread and serious social phenomenon following in the wake of urban dislocation. It is likely to increase social and psychological "pathology" in a limited number of instances, and it is also likely to create new opportunities for some, and to increase the rate of social mobility for others. For the greatest number, dislocation is unlikely to have either effect but does lead to intense personal suffering despite moderately successful adaptation to the total situation of relocation.[5]

In short, these sociologists pointed out that substandard housing was not necessarily an unmitigated evil to those who lived in it.

The second side attacking the reformers' case for public housing as a means of relocating slum dwellers questioned the whole relationship of poor housing to slums. Indeed, numerous indicators of social pathology did (and do) correlate with substandard housing. But correlation does not imply causation; and public housing—or

---

[4] Lee Rainwater, "Fear and the House-As-Haven in the Lower Class," Bellush and Hausknecht, op. cit. (n. 1), p. 437.

[5] Marc Fried, "Grieving for a Lost Home," Urban Renewal: The Record and the Controversy, ed., James W. Wilson (Cambridge: MIT Press, 1966), p. 376.

the diminution in various ways of structurally substandard housing —has not brought about by itself any significant improvement in the social pathology of low-income people. As John Dean comments:

The implication (of the housing reformers) is: "Remove the slums and you remove the social ills." But it would be just as illogical to say that ills of slum areas are caused not by substandard housing conditions, but by the absence of telephone service, which also correlates with indexes [sic] of social disorder. . . . Beyond a few expected relationships between slum dwellings and health, the effect of poor housing becomes quite difficult to determine where social behavior is involved.[6]

Of course this does not mean that housing as a variable is unimportant or has no effect. It does mean that the destruction of slum housing per se and the housing of all people in standard housing will not necessarily usher in the millennium. This seemingly obvious argument has been oftentimes ignored, until recently, by some of the original housing reformers from the 1930's.

Though substandard housing is quite often present in slums, a slum is not determined by the existence (or presence) of substandard housing. Rather, it is a community with a significant percentage of its inhabitants living in poverty. In this study, poverty is viewed as a cycle consisting of a mutually reenforcing set of deprivations associated with inadequate income. The deprivations are mutually reenforcing in that one disability reenforces another, which in turn makes the original disability all the more difficult to overcome. The deprivations, in short, are not separate and distinct, but are intimately connected with one another, so that it is difficult to deal successfully with one deprivation without dealing with a whole cluster of them.[7]

From the above discussion it becomes clear that housing all poverty-stricken people in standard housing is not by itself going to

[6] Dean, *op. cit.* (n. 2), p. 28.

[7] For a more complete discussion of this point see the author's "Towards an Understanding of Poverty"—a first draft prepared at the Washington Center for Metropolitan Studies in Washington, D.C.

end poverty (and, therefore, the slums). Indeed, without attacking other deprivations at the same time, it is quite possible that the result will be quick deterioration of structurally standard housing at the hands of many of the inhabitants. Poor housing, thus, is one of the set of mutually reenforcing deprivations in the vicious cycle of poverty—and quite probably not the most important one. This does not mean that efforts directed at improving housing for the poor are useless. Although the poverty cycle cannot be broken easily, the cumulative effect of poverty can be lightened by improved housing.

A multitude of studies have established the common-sense relationship between poor housing and poor health. Diseases related to inadequate or malfunctioning sanitary conditions and injuries related to deteriorating facilities (stairs, poor electrical conditions, etc.) are easily seen to be directly linked to substandard housing. In addition, inadequacy of internal space—overcrowding—is clearly related to poor mental health and increased psychological stress.[8] Other causal relationships are not nearly so clear or direct. Alvin Schorr, who has done a comprehensive review of the literature on this problem, concludes:

The type of housing occupied influences health, behavior, and attitude, particularly if the housing is desperately inadequate. In terms that we use today, "desperately inadequate" means that housing is dilapidated or lacks a major facility such as running water. . . .

Housing, even when it is minimally adequate, appears to influence family and social relationships. Other influences of adequate housing are uncertain. . . . Those influences on behavior and attitudes that have been established bear a relationship to whether people can move out of or stay out of poverty. The following effects may spring from poor housing: a perception of one's self that leads to pessimism and passivity, stress to which the individual cannot adapt, poor health, and a state of dissatisfaction; pleasure in company but not in solitude, cynicism about people and organizations, a high degree of sexual stimulation without legitimate outlet, and difficulty in household management and child-rearing; and rela-

[8] Schorr, *op. cit.* (n. 3), pp. 16–17.

tionships that tend to spread out in the neighborhood rather than deeply into the family. Most of these effects, in turn, place obstacles in the path of improving one's financial position.[9]

Again, this is not to say that poor housing "causes" these behaviors and attitudes which comprise a part (but certainly not the whole) of the poverty cycle. Rather, poor housing contributes, in many cases quite significantly, to these results. Thus improved housing would serve to lessen some of the deprivations associated with poverty. By itself, housing improvement will not end the slums.

## The Housing Stock

What is the condition of the housing stock in this country? By strict structural standards, there is little doubt that it has consistently improved over the last several decades. Both in percentage and absolute terms, the number of substandard houses—as measured by nearly any set of consistent structural standards—has fallen. How to interpret this improvement, most of which is due simply to the natural operations of the housing market rather than to any specific government program or programs, is quite another matter. Like poverty, substandard housing is better understood as a relative concept rather than an absolute one. What was an acceptable housing unit fifty or twenty-five years ago may be considered substandard now. The term "substandard" is not only relative to the times, but also to environmental surroundings. As Sergei Grimm points out, "Substandard is whatever is worst in *our neighborhood*."[10] In this sense—and in policy terms, the most meaningful sense—substandard housing is not an objective standard, but a value judgment.

In view of this, it may not come as much of a surprise to learn that the Census Bureau, which conducts a decennial Census of

[9] *Ibid.*, pp. 31–32.

[10] Scott Greer, *Urban Renewal and American Cities* (New York: Bobbs-Merrill, 1965), p. 22.

Housing, collects no data on any category termed "substandard housing." Instead, the Census Bureau in 1960 divided the housing stock into three categories—sound, deteriorating, and dilapidated —in order to describe structural conditions.[11] Within the first two categories, the Census Bureau further subdivided the housing stock into sound or deteriorating; with all plumbing facilities, lacking only hot water, or lacking private toilet or bath or running water. On the other hand, the Public Housing Administration, formerly a constituent agency of Housing and Home Finance Agency (HHFA) and now called the Housing Assistance Administration, does make use of the term "substandard housing" and subsumes

[11] *Sound* housing is defined as that which has no defects, or only slight defects which normally are corrected during the course of regular maintenance. Examples of slight defects are: lack of paint; slight damage to porch or steps; slight wearing away of mortar between bricks or other masonry; small cracks in walls, plaster, or chimney; cracked windows; slight wear on floors, doorsills, doorframes, window sills, or window frames; and broken gutters or downspouts.

*Deteriorating* housing needs more repair than would be provided in the course of regular maintenance. Such housing has one or more defects of an intermediate nature that must be corrected if the unit is to continue to provide safe and adequate shelter. Examples of intermediate defects are: holes, open cracks, rotted, loose, or missing material over a small area of the foundation, walls, roof, floors, or ceilings; shaky or unsafe porch, steps, or railings; several broken or missing windowpanes; some rotted or loose window frames or sashes that are no longer rainproof or windproof; broken or loose stair treads, or broken, loose, or missing risers, balusters, or railings of inside or outside stairs; deep wear on doorsills, doorframes, outside or inside steps or floors; missing bricks or cracks in the chimney which are not serious enough to be a fire hazard; and makeshift chimney such as a stovepipe or other uninsulated pipe leading directly from the stove to the outside through a hole in the roof, walls, or window. Such defects are signs of neglect which lead to serious structural deterioration or damage if not corrected.

*Dilapidated* housing does not provide safe and adequate shelter and its present condition endangers the health, safety, or well-being of the occupants. Such housing has one or more critical defects, or has a combination of intermediate defects in sufficient number or extent to require considerable repair or rebuilding, or is of inadequate original construction. The defects are either so critical or so widespread that the structure should be extensively repaired, rebuilt, or torn down.

*Critical defects* result from continued neglect or lack of repair, or indicate serious damage to the structure. Examples of critical defects are: holes, open cracks, or rotted, loose, or missing material (clapboard siding, shingles, bricks, concrete, tile, plaster, or floorboards) *over a large area* of the foundation, out-under that category all dilapidated housing, plus all sound or deteriorating housing with inadequate plumbing facilities.[12] Note that under the categories both of the Census Bureau and of the Housing Assistance Administration, overcrowding is not considered a factor in substandard housing nor is excessive rent. The Census terms deal only with the physical quality of housing units and not with the people who may live in them.

If we use Census categories we find that fully three-quarters of the housing stock in the country is sound with all plumbing facilities and that 80 percent of the stock inside SMSA's (Standard Metropolitan Statistical Areas) compared to only 61 percent outside these areas belongs in that category. On the whole, housing is better, as these statistics indicate, in cities and suburbs, worse in small towns and rural areas. The South, with only 30 percent of the housing units in the country, had nearly 50 percent of the units which were dilapidated or lacked proper plumbing facilities. Rental housing was apt to be in poorer condition than owner-occupied housing (66 percent of rental units were sound with proper plumbing facilities compared to 83 percent of owner-occupied dwellings). And, as might be guessed, nonwhites were deprived by a larger margin than whites (only 53 percent of owner-occupied nonwhite dwellings and 39 percent of rental units occupied by nonwhites were sound with all plumbing facilities).[13]

---

side walls, roof, chimney, or inside walls, floors, or ceilings; substantial sagging of floors, walls, or roof; and extensive damage by storm, fire, or flood.

To be classified as dilapidated on the basis of intermediate defects, a housing unit must have such defects in sufficient number or extent that it no longer provides safe and adequate shelter. No set number of intermediate defects is required.

*Inadequate original construction* includes: shacks, huts, or tents; structures with makeshift walls or roofs, or built of packing boxes, scrap lumber, or tin; structures lacking foundations (walls rest directly on the ground); structures with dirt floors; and cellars, sheds, barns, garages, or other places not originally intended for living quarters and inadequately converted to such use.

[12] Leonore R. Siegelman, "A Technical Note on Housing Census Comparability, 1950–60," *Journal of the American Institute of Planners,* XXIX (February, 1963), 51–52.

[13] Glenn Beyer, *Housing and Society* (New York: Macmillan Company, 1966), pp. 122–125.

If we add overcrowding to structural deficiencies and plumbing deficiencies as an element of "substandard" housing, we find, according to Nathan Glazer, that 21 percent of nonfarm families are ill-housed, as are 37 percent of those earning under $4,000, 53 percent of those with nonwhite heads of families, and 65 percent of nonwhite families with incomes under $4,000.[14]

## Housing and Low-Income People

Why are so many poor people inadequately housed? The not so startling answer is that they lack the income necessary to purchase good housing. Schorr, writing in 1963, reports studies which demonstrate that a family cannot expect to obtain adequate housing unless its income is above $5,000–$6,000 per year.[15] The Bureau of Labor Statistics suggests that a family ought to spend about 20 percent of its income on housing. Unfortunately, for incomes under $5,000, it is exceedingly difficult to obtain standard housing on the market by spending only 20 percent of income. The choices available to such a family are reduced to obtaining adequate housing at the expense of deficiencies in other necessities such as food and clothing or to accept inadequate housing. One oft-used strategy is to cut housing costs by doubling up families in single-family dwellings with, of course, resultant overcrowding.

In economic terms, it is rather difficult to generalize from one area to another about the low-income housing market, or, indeed, about the housing market itself. The overriding fact about the housing market in this country is that there is really no such thing. Rather there are housing *markets*, each one largely independent of others in different localities. Within each local housing market there are various submarkets, many of which are also nearly independent from one another, in the sense that a prospective buyer in one submarket would not consider a dwelling in other submarkets.

[14] Nathan Glazer, "Housing Problems and Housing Policies," *The Public Interest*, VII (Spring 1967), 21.

[15] Schorr, *op. cit.* (n. 3), p. 98.

Thus one market might be based on structure (single-family vs. apartment or row houses), another on tenure (owner-occupancy vs. rental), still another on value level or rental rates (low-income, middle-income, or high-income), and finally one on locational criteria (type of neighborhood being sought).

What can be said about the low-income housing submarket generally? Although the submarket will vary greatly from city to city, it seems safe to say that the supply is predominantly rental and overwhelmingly part of the standing stock. Owner-occupancy in the low-income submarket is not widespread in most cities, for the obvious reason that the kind of terms the poor would need for ownership are not readily available.[16] Nearly all of the new rental housing is being built for the middle-income submarket or above. In these submarkets it is possible to charge sufficient rents to realize a handsome return on investment; such is not the case in the low-income submarket.

Most low-income families are therefore dependent for accommodations upon rental housing obtained through the filtering process. R. U. Ratcliff defines "filtering" as "the changing of occupancy [which occurs] as the housing that is occupied by one income group becomes available to the next lower-income group as a result in the decline of market price, i.e., in sales price or rent value."[17] Filtering thus results from new construction at any income level as higher-income groups abandon older housing to groups with lower income. Unfortunately, particularly with rental housing, the result is often obsolescent or deteriorating housing filtering down to low-income groups.

The problems of the filtering process are, of course, greatly exacerbated in many cities by the existence of rigidly segregated housing markets. This greatly narrows the housing opportunities open to Negroes and results in greater demand and higher rentals if the

[16] Charles Abrams, *The City is the Frontier* (New York: Harper and Row, 1965), p. 285.

[17] William Grigsby, *Housing Markets and Public Policy* (Philadelphia: University of Pennsylvania Press, 1963), p. 86.

market is tight or lower maintenance standards and deteriorating housing if the market is loose. In a tight market rents will likely be high (relative to ability to pay) and the vacancy rate low as excess demand bids up the price for housing. In a loose market landlords dare not raise rents, for fear of losing tenants. Instead they are likely to cut services and maintenance in an attempt to cut costs and thus increase profits.

It is worth noting at this point that the relatively high rents and low maintenance in the low-income submarket are not due solely to cold-hearted slumlords. Hard financial and economic considerations also lead in the same direction.

Slum landlords justify their high rate of profit as necessary because of the risk involved. Presumably if expected returns were not so high, landlords would find alternative investments at lower risks and the supply and quality of low-income rental housing would be even lower than it is now. In a brilliant study of slum landlords in Newark (where the market is loose), George Sternlieb concludes:

It is the risk factor . . . which raises the required threshold of return on investment in slum properties. . . . The high rate of current return demanded by investors in slum tenements can be summarized as a compound of the fear of costly code crackdowns; the basic weakness of the market, both in terms of rental increases, and securing full tenancy; the risk of outright loss through the complete abandonment of a parcel; and in substantial part, the pejoratives which society heaps upon the "slumlord." [18]

The filtering process is particularly ineffective if new construction lags. The result in such an event would be an inadequate supply of housing, much of it in not very good shape, available to the poor.

In this situation rehabilitation of existing dwelling units has been called for as the answer to the housing problems of the poor.

[18] George Sternlieb, *The Tenement Landlord* (New Brunswick, N.J.: The William Byrd Press Inc., 1966), pp. 95–96.

What are the barriers to success in this approach? There are several. First, according to Sternlieb, it is difficult for any but large holders of slum properties to obtain the necessary financing for rehabilitation. Then, too, many landlords are hesitant to rehabilitate because rehabilitation requires higher rents, and this is impossible if the market is loose. If the market is tight, however, rehabilitation will mean higher rents for tenants who cannot afford them. In this situation it is unlikely rehabilitation will serve the needs of the lower classes without, at the same time, some form of rent subsidization.

Another barrier to rehabilitation is the fear of landlords that their improved property will be reassessed with resulting high taxes. Sternlieb observes that sheer ignorance, both of what a reassessable improvement is and how to go about obtaining rehabilitation financing, are major factors in the lack of impact rehabilitation has thus far made.[19] He also points to another problem with rehabilitation efforts that too often is ignored: "A basic problem of slum maintenance and rehabilitation is the attitude of tenantry, largely a function of their basic alienation from the absentee landlord. Any effort towards rehabilitation which does not face up to this reality is pure romanticism."[20]

In short, except where strict code enforcement is a definite possibility, most landlords perceive that they have little to gain and possibly a good deal to lose (increased vacancy rates in loose markets, or if rent is not raised, decreased return). And code enforcement has been notoriously ineffective in nearly all American cities, in part because codes are unrealistically strict. If all code violations were required to be eliminated, many landlords would probably sell or abandon their holdings rather than undertake costly improvements to themselves unless they could be assured either of subsidy or of successfully passing the costs on to the tenantry without increasing vacancy rates.

[19] *Ibid.*, p. xv.
[20] *Ibid.*

### The Authoritative Allocation of Values—
### Housing and the Political System:
### Federal Housing Administration

The federal government's major response to housing problems arose out of the Great Depression experience. It was a response to a problem which was qualitatively different from the problem of housing perceived by those who today refer to "the housing problem." Housing construction is an industry which is one of the first to suffer during an economic downturn. During the Depression it not only suffered first, but also suffered most. The FHA mortgage insurance program which came out of the National Housing Act of 1934 was therefore primarily a response to the collapsed condition of the housing industry. Sherman Maisel explains FHA as an effort

to reduce the risks of the mortgage market in order to make savings institutions lend more willingly on real estate. This increased lending would foster a step-up in building, more employment, and an increase in the gross national product. The failure of the housing industry to re-establish itself was recognized as a major drag on the entire economy. From its start, the FHA was concerned with influencing the level of housing production.[21]

FHA mortgage insurance, as the name implies, is insurance provided by the federal government to the lending institution. In other words, the risk of nonpayment and foreclosure is assumed by the government rather than the lending agency. All FHA loans must be approved by the local FHA office in accordance with certain standards set by the FHA Commissioner. Included in these standards is one requiring that the interest charge must be below a specified maximum rate (usually very close to the market rate) set by the Commissioner. The loans must also be made on the basis of a minimum downpayment and repaid within a maximum specified time period, again set by the Commissioner. These specified regu-

[21] Sherman J. Maisel, *Financing Real Estate* (New York: McGraw-Hill, 1965), p. 100.

lations have been progressively liberalized since 1934. The major advantage to the home buyer from FHA mortgage insurance has thus been less required downpayment and a longer period for repayment rather than reduced interest rates.

One further regulation not changed until 1967 was that the loans be based on the criteria of "economic soundness." This meant that attempts to make use of FHA insurance in slum areas have failed because of the "excessive risk" involved in extending loans to low-income people in a deteriorating area. FHA, which operates on a decentralized local basis, has developed quite good relations with local financial institutions, and its lending policy reflects the same conservative direction that characterizes its clientele. Because of this, it has gained the reputation of an institution not readily sympathetic to the needs of the poor.

Indeed, the housing needs of low-income families have not been well served by FHA. In addition to the difficulty in showing "economic soundness" on loans to low-income individuals, interest costs are still generally too high, relative to incomes of the poor. Poor families would need some kind of mortgage subsidy in order to consider buying. Such a provision (Sec. 235) was a major part of the housing legislation which Congress passed in 1968.

Section 235 provides for a mortgage subsidy which in some cases would leave the buyer only 1 percent interest to pay. Even this program, however, does not reach many with poverty-level income. FHA mortgage insurance for rental housing has had a similarly miniscule effect so far as aiding low-income families is concerned.

Thus, in 1964, only 2.4 percent of FHA loans on homes (Sec. 203) went to families with an income under $4,800 per year; and only 0.3 percent of apartments built with FHA guarantees rented for less than $100 a month (which would require a $4,800 per year income if it is assumed a family can spend 25 percent of its income on rent). Section 236, the Rental Housing Assistance Program which became law in 1968, was designed to reorder FHA priorities. Like Section 235 it relies on a mortgage subsidy to cut the landlord's costs and thus provide lower rents for tenants. A special provision in the legislation allows residents of 235 apartments also to receive rent supplements thereby opening up Section 235 housing to low-income families.

FHA insurance has had a major impact on middle and lower-middle income families over the past three decades. In many ways it has provided the financing mechanism to move young families from the city to owner-occupied homes in the suburbs, where FHA has had its greatest impact. Indeed, surveys over a three-year period (1964–66) show that about two-thirds of FHA housing within SMSA's has been in the suburbs.

The rate of homeownership has, in fact, soared since 1945. But this process has generally benefited low-income families, if at all, only through the filtering mechanism by which dwelling units are made available in the city as they are abandoned by more affluent families migrating to the suburbs. Recently efforts have increased, with some success, at orienting FHA more towards the problems of poor people. FHA is the agency, for example, which administers the rent supplement program as well as both new mortgage subsidy programs Sections 235 and 236.

## Housing and the Political System: Public Housing

The New Deal's other major response to "the housing problem" again seems curiously outdated in terms of what we perceive today under that name. That many people were poorly housed during the thirties was not only recognized by housing experts but was the subject of public discussion. Franklin Roosevelt's "one-third of a nation" speech is an eloquent testimony to public concern. But the problem was *not* viewed, at that time, as primarily an urban Negro problem, a factor which was to bedevil the government's housing efforts in later years. At the same time, much of the concern about easily visible slums was not about the deprivations suffered by their inhabitants, but rather about the affront to aesthetic sensibilities caused by these blights on the urban landscape.

The government's response to these considerations clearly reflected the Depression atmosphere in which it was shaped. It is not surprising, therefore, that the first slum clearance and public housing program, initiated in 1933, was administered by the Public Works Administration. The program was aimed primarily at stimulating the economy; other objectives were secondary or incidental. This was stated very clearly by Harold Ickes, who outlined the goals of the PWA housing program as: "First to deal with the unemployment situation by giving employment to workers. . . . Second, to furnish decent, sanitary dwellings to those whose incomes are so low that private capital is unable to provide adequate housing within their means. Third to eradicate and rehabilitate slum areas. . . ." [22]

The PWA experiment served as the basis for a much larger and permanent public housing program. In 1937 Congress passed the Wagner-Steagall Low Rent Housing Bill, which established the United States Housing Authority. The bill was passed over the protests of Congressmen who saw the road to socialism clearly leading from the doorstep of public housing.

Unlike earlier public housing efforts, the USHA was to work through local public housing agencies, which in turn would own and control (consistent with a set of federal regulations which quickly burgeoned to mammoth proportions) the housing projects. Local public agencies were eligible for long-term 60-year loans for up to 90 percent of the costs of financing the housing projects. (The long-term loan means a lower amortization, which in turn means lower rentals.) In addition, the agencies were to receive a grant in aid from the federal government covering the difference between the economic rents of a project (the rents necessary to cover cost if the project were unsubsidized) and the social rents (the rents the lowest-income group can afford to pay). [23]

[22] Jewell Bellush and Murray Hausknecht, "Urban Renewal: An Historical Overview," Bellush and Hausknecht, *op. cit.* (n. 1), p. 7.
[23] Charles Abrams, *The Future of Housing* (New York: Harper and Brothers, 1946), p. 260.

Despite the fact that the projects had to be initiated, approved, and operated by local authorities, the federal requirements to be fulfilled were quite rigorous. They included specifications for the physical structure of the project (rooms not to exceed certain size, etc.), and income limitations on inhabitants (both maximum and minimum) as well as required local contributions (10 percent of the cost of building and 20 percent of the annual federal subsidy). In addition there was a requirement that for each unit of public housing erected, a slum dwelling unit had to be torn down.[24]

Although this last proviso was not strictly enforced, it testifies eloquently to the fact that the original objectives of public housing were as much to tear down ugly slums as to improve housing opportunities for poor people. An effort to achieve the latter would have left all but the most dangerous slum dwellings standing at the same time as public housing went up, in an effort to bring down the level of rents by increasing supply in the low-income submarket.

What has public housing accomplished? Under the Housing Act of 1937, some 114,000 units of public housing were built. The Housing Act of 1949 authorized an additional 810,000 units of housing to be built over a six-year period. Public housing during the 1930's and 1940's indeed was seen by most housing experts as the ultimate solution to the housing problems of the poor. One of the most sophisticated of these, Charles Abrams, concluded in 1946: "We must look ahead to the days when perhaps a quarter or a third of our population will be living in public projects." [25]

It is difficult to imagine anyone making such a statement today. Public housing has become an unpopular program even among many liberals, its early sponsors. Congress has consistently refused to appropriate high levels of funds and as a result, of the 810,000 units authorized in 1949 to be built in six years, only 670,000 had been completed by the end of 1969 (see Appendix 4). Moreover, as Robert Ellickson concludes, recent public housing projects have

[24] *Ibid.*, p. 261.
[25] *Ibid.*, p. 371.

ceased to perform any meaningful function so far as nonelderly low-income city residents are concerned. "Of the 26,000 new units constructed annually (as of 1966), about half are designed exclusively for the *elderly* and many of the rest are located in small towns just beginning participation in the program. The program no longer provides much new housing for the non-elderly low-income families living in urban ghettos." [26]

Why has traditional public housing been, as Nathan Glazer has called it, "a graveyard of good intentions"? [27] The foremost reason is that the perceived beneficiaries have changed, in much the same way as has happened with other social welfare programs of the New Deal era. Gilbert Steiner, in his study of welfare policy, quotes Frank Bane, an early director of the Social Security Board, concerning the New Deal vision of the ADC (Aid to Dependent Children) recipient: "The ADC example we always thought about," Bane remarked, "was the poor lady in West Virginia whose husband was killed in a mining accident, and the problem of how she could feed those kids." [28]

"ADC money," Steiner comments, "is now going to recipients with very different characteristics from the recipient group of the depression. As a matter of fact, the whole public relief program now deals with recipients with different characteristics from those of recipients of the depression period." [29] The same, indeed, holds true with public housing recipients. In the Depression years, public housing beneficiaries were perceived to be, as Alvin Schorr notes, "families who voluntarily sought to improve their housing but could not afford private rentals. This group was not regarded as dependent." [30] If anything, it was seen to be a cross section of the American population. More recently, the image of the public

[26] Robert Ellickson, "Government Housing Assistance to the Poor," *Yale Law Review,* LXXVI, No. 3 (January, 1967), 511–512.

[27] Glazer, *op. cit.* (n. 14), p. 35.

[28] Gilbert Steiner, *Social Insecurity: The Politics of Welfare* (Chicago: Rand McNally, 1966), p. 237.

[29] *Ibid.,* p. 33.

[30] Schorr, *op. cit.* (n. 3), p. 110.

housing family has changed. Public housing is perceived to consist of a relatively high concentration of depressed, untutored, and dependent families. And most of these are thought to be Negro.[31]

Anxiety on the part of many relatively affluent Americans that public housing might mean low-income Negro families living next door to them in projects has accounted for both fewer units of public housing (as this anxiety has communicated itself to Congressmen) and the high concentration of what public housing there is in slum areas.

Public housing has also suffered because it has disproven for all to see the old theory that physical housing structure is the main cause of slums. Many, if not most, public housing projects have merely relocated the slum environment, not changed it. The shock with which many New Deal liberals faced this fact is registered in Harrison Salisbury's account of his tour of New York in 1958. It is worth quoting at length:

I have been away from the United States a good deal since the War. When I came back to New York and drove the expressway around the island I hardly recognized parts of the city. The great experiment in public housing launched during the Roosevelt administration seemed to have paid off. I was amazed at the changes. Whole areas of the city had given way to fine new construction. I wished that I could take a delegation of Russians around and show them what a magnificent job we were doing in the field of public housing.

Then, last winter I visited Fort Greene Houses, Brooklyn. . . .

Until my nostrils ferreted out the fetid story of Fort Greene and until I had seen the inside of Mercy Houses and St. Nicholas Houses I was not aware that in too many instances we have merely institutionalized our slums. We have immured old horror and new deprivation behind these cold walls. . . .

Fort Greene projects . . . are fiendishly contrived institutions for the debasing of family and community life to the lowest common mean. They are worse than anything George Orwell conceived.[32]

---

[31] Actually about 50 percent of public housing families are Negro. See Ellickson, *op. cit.* (n. 26), p. 511.

[32] Harrison Salisbury, "The Shook-up Generation," Bellush and Hausknecht, *op. cit.* (n. 1), pp. 426–427.

Salisbury, of course, overreacted. Public housing projects no more "cause" slums (debase family and community life) than they could eliminate slums. But how much have the projects contributed to better housing for the poor? Much recent criticism from the political left has suggested that public housing represents an abhorrent symbol to the poor and is chosen only as a last resort. Schorr quotes several studies which indicate that there is, among a large segment of the poor, a decided reluctance to reside in public housing.[33] On the other hand, he also cites several studies which show that a majority of those who *do* live in public housing say they like it and exhibit higher morale than they did in their previous substandard housing.[34] And however unsatisfactory public housing is, every city has huge waiting lists of families trying desperately to get into an inadequate supply.

Public housing is undoubtedly unpleasant to the poor compared to other alternatives which are not realistically open to them. Like most slums, it is a meeting place for antisocial behavior and crime; particularly in a high-rise project, individual antisocial behavior (urinating in the elevator is always cited) is likely to impinge on the entire community. Then, too, tenants are circumscribed by a set of bureaucratic regulations, each one, no doubt, well-meaning in intention, but often suffocating and counterproductive in aggregate. Undoubtedly, the *most* counterproductive was the regulation (recent attempts have been made to modify it) which required tenants to move out once their incomes exceeded the maximum limit. Not only did this act to impede initiative (it may be difficult to find comparable housing even with a slightly higher income), but it had the effect of systematically removing the most stable and active members of the project.

Finally, public housing has become entangled in its own bureaucratic mechanisms. It takes a seemingly interminable length of time and miles of red tape to get a project approved and constructed. An exchange during the 1965 Rent Supplement hearings

[33] Schorr, *op. cit.* (n. 3), p. 64.
[34] *Ibid.*, p. 115.

between Senator Douglas (D–Ill.) and Nathaniel S. Keith, President of the National Housing Conference, generally speaking, the lobby group for local housing bureaucrats, is revealing here.

SEN. DOUGLAS: The staff calls my attention to the fact that there were 24,000 units constructed last year. . . . That 24,000 sounds extraordinarily low. We have been authorizing 35,000 year after year after year, and I have always thought that ceiling was too low, but when the ceiling is not taken advantage of . . .

Now you show vigorous reaction so far as making a claim, but will the local agencies show equal vigor in performance? I think you ought to read the riot act to your members.

MR. KEITH: I think that is sound advice, Senator.

SEN. DOUGLAS: Go ahead.

MR. KEITH: In keeping with what we have been discussing the last few moments, we are recommending that the authorization be increased 125,000 units a year.

SEN. DOUGLAS: Well, that is fine, but will you see the local units build the 35,000 that have been authorized in these past years?

SEN. SPARKMAN: By the way, we had the same experience back when we were operating under the 135,000 a year. It never did come up, I believe, more than, I guess, 75,000 in one year.

MR. KEITH: I think that was about the maximum rate. Then, of course, there was the fact that during the 1950's and for several years, the Appropriations Committee—

SEN. DOUGLAS: Part of the fault is due to Congress, there is no doubt about that. But certainly some of the fault must lie in the localities.

MR. KEITH: I have to agree with you on that.

SEN. DOUGLAS: Good for you. Now what can your association do?

MR. KEITH: Well, I don't know. I guess we have to do more than we have in the past.[35]

If public housing is going to serve any useful future function, it is generally acknowledged that significant innovations must occur. Recent attempts at making the program more flexible seem to have had some degree of success, although they have not, as yet, gener-

---

[35] U. S. Congress, Senate Subcommittee on Housing, Committee on Banking and Currency, *Hearings, Housing Legislation of 1965*, 89th Cong., 1st Sess. (1965), pp. 266–69.

ated a significant volume of public housing (see Appendix 5). These new attempts at innovation include provisions for tenants to purchase their units should their income permit them to do so. Other programs allow for local authorities to purchase and rehabilitate existing housing for use as public housing (flexible formula) and for the authority to rent existing housing as public housing, paying rent subsidies to the landlord on behalf of the public housing tenant who lives there (the Widnall plan). A final promising approach is "turnkey," in which private builders, rather than the housing authority itself, develop new projects and then sell them to local authorities. The result has been both cheaper and quicker than the traditional approach. One barrier to these innovations is the attitude of the traditional public housing bureaucracy (as represented by the National Association of Housing and Redevelopment Officials—NAHRO), which has a vested interest in the continuance of the large public housing projects they have constructed and managed since the 1930's.[36]

The fact is, however, that public housing does not seem likely to make future contributions for two reasons. First, very few people are pushing it as a vitally important program the way they were in the 1930's. Second, and more important, Congress is unlikely to grant large sums of money for public housing so long as fear persists among whites that public housing may mean Negroes in their community. That this fear has largely been groundless (there have been very few projects moving Negroes into white areas) [37] does not belie the fact that the fear exists. In short, the character of the opposition to public housing has changed. One seldom hears arguments now against public housing in terms of so-

[36] Verrick O. French, a research associate at the Washington Center for Metropolitan Studies during the time this study was being conducted, told of the suspicion with which the local public housing authority viewed his evaluation of the Widnall Plan housing program in Washington. His evaluation was that the program was a great success. (Personal interview, August 8, 1967.)

[37] A 1969 court decision in Chicago which requires that public housing be built in all areas of the city rather than solely in Negro ghettos, will lend some reality to this perception, if it is effectively implemented.

cialism, but rather in terms of social engineering by the government or of "forcing integration."

## Housing and the Political System: Urban Renewal

Congress passed the Housing Act of 1949 with a ringing declaration of federal policy. The preamble to that Act stated:

The Congress hereby declares that the general welfare and security of the Nation and the health and living standards of its people require housing production and related community development sufficient to remedy the serious housing shortage, the elimination of substandard and other inadequate housing through the clearance of slums and blighted areas, and the realization as soon as feasible of the goal of a decent home and suitable living environment for every American family, thus contributing to the development and redevelopment of communities and to the advancement of the growth, wealth, and security of the Nation.

—Housing Act of 1949 [38]

The Act had two main features. Title I covered slum clearance and urban redevelopment. Title III provided for 810,000 units of low-rent public housing in which, it was assumed, those families which would be uprooted by slum clearance could be rehoused (indeed the Act gave such displacees preferences in public housing). The first title provided federal loans to a local public agency for assembly, clearance, and site preparation of blighted land. The prepared land was then to be sold by the city to private concerns which would develop the area in accordance with a redevelopment plan. The most important provision of the Act specified that the federal government would pay two-thirds of the cost of the city's loss if the cost of buying and preparing the land exceeded the gains of selling it to the developer (as it invariably did). The result, of course, enabled private developers to obtain land from cities at a very substantial write-down of its actual cost with the difference being subsidized by the United States government.

[38] *Housing a Nation* (Washington, D.C.: *Congressional Quarterly*, 1966), p. 28.

The 1949 Housing Act was passed in a period of severe housing shortage; and it appears clear, as the preamble suggests, that Congress intended a major purpose of the legislation to be the provision of housing for the poor on the cleared sites. Thus, Ashley Foard and Hilbert Fefferman, two HHFA lawyers who were involved in drawing up the legislation, observe that Senator Taft (R–Ohio), the chief proponent of the bill, "questioned the federal interest in any project going 'beyond housing and beyond the elimination of slums.' He argued that the federal government was committed to a policy of assisting housing, thereby relieving poverty and hardship, and that federally-aided urban redevelopment for this social welfare purpose was desirable, but projects going further merely improved the looks or financial status of local communities." [39]

If this, indeed, was the intent of Congress, it has been quite consistently flouted. Most urban renewal projects have *not* provided housing for low-income families, because such an effort would not be a profit-rewarding one for the private developer who undertook it. Rather, most projects have resulted in middle or upper-middle income apartment housing and/or commercial development. Indeed it is not unfair to say that urban renewal has worked as a detriment to the poor rather than as an aid. It is their houses which are uprooted and it is they who are moved from the renewal neighborhood, where the new rents are no longer within their ability to pay. They must be relocated and relocation efforts have not been especially successful. Originally it was thought that relocation would occur in the 810,000 units of public housing authorized in the 1949 Act. However, as has been noted, nearly twenty years later, the full 810,000 units are still not completed. Instead, all too often, the poor who were displaced simply have moved into slum housing in other parts of the city, housing only marginally better and often more expensive than that which they previously occupied. And, since for the most part inhabitants of central city slum

[39] Ashley A. Foard and Hilbert Fefferman, "Federal Urban Renewal Legislation," Wilson, *op. cit.* (n. 5), p. 105.

areas subject to renewal have been Negro, it is no wonder that urban renewal is referred to by many bitter slum dwellers as "Negro removal." Chester Hartman, who has conducted a detailed study of relocation efforts from renewal areas, reports: "It is an inescapable conclusion that relocation has been only an ancillary component of the renewal process; were this not the case, the community would find totally unacceptable 'slum clearance' projects which leave as many as two-thirds of the displaced families still living in substandard conditions, or which actually increase the incidence of overcrowding." [40]

The Omnibus Housing Act of 1954 was aimed at accelerating the pace of urban redevelopment as well as rectifying some of the more glaring difficulties with the 1949 legislation. Apparently, incentives had not been high enough in the 1949 Act, for in the first five-year period after passage, only sixty cities had reached even the land acquisition stage. In the most optimistic words of its own administrators, the program had merely "gained momentum." [41]

As a result, in the 1954 Act several important changes were made. First, in Title I the term "urban renewal" was substituted for "urban redevelopment," and the concept was broadened to include restoration and rehabilitation in accordance with an urban renewal plan rather than simply clearance. A section (220) was added to the National Housing Act of 1937 making available, on liberal terms, FHA mortgage money for new or rehabilitated sales and rental housing in urban renewal areas. In addition, Section 221 authorized FHA mortgage insurance aid for displaced families seeking relocation anywhere in the community. However, neither of these changes has had any significant impact on low-income families. As has already been pointed out, tinkering with the mortgage terms is likely to have only a minor effect on the housing choices open to poverty-level families—the cost of good housing is still likely to be too high for many without additional subsidy.

Section 220, making FHA mortgage money available for housing

---

[40] Chester Hartman, "The Housing of Relocated Families," *ibid.*, p. 321.
[41] Abrams, *The City is the Frontier, op. cit.* (n. 23), p. 86.

in urban renewal areas, was not even aimed primarily at the poor. Thus, Foard and Fefferman comment: "Because the purpose of section 220 is to encourage renewal of project areas for their most suitable housing use, WHICH IS NOT NECESSARILY LOW-INCOME HOUSING [caps mine], section 220 insured mortgages may be considerably larger in amount per dwelling unit than mortgages insured under 221, which is designed to serve displaced persons who are generally of low or moderate income." [41a] Section 220, at any rate, has accounted for only a little more than 60,000 units of housing since its inception. (At the end of 1966, the entire omnibus housing program had generated 216,600 units of new or rehabilitated housing.)

At the same time the Act of 1954 made the first exemption in a requirement written into the 1949 Act which required that a project area must be either predominantly residential in character to begin with or redeveloped for primarily residential use. The history of the erosion of this residential requirement since 1949 is best stated by HUD itself:

Nonresidential renewal.—The 1954 exception to the predominantly residential requirement of title I was limited to 10 percent of capital grant funds and was also limited to areas containing a substantial number of substandard living accommodations. The exception has been changed several times. It now provides that 30 percent of the aggregate amount of Federal grants authorized for contracting on or after the enactment of the Housing Act of 1959 may be made available under the exception, along with 35 percent of the amount of capital grants authorized for contracting on or after the enactment of the Housing and Urban Development Act of 1965. Also, the requirement that there must be a substantial number of substandard dwellings has been dropped, and in its place, there has been enacted a requirement that redevelopment for predominantly non-residential uses shall have been found by the locality to be "necessary for the proper development of the community." [42]

[41a] Foard and Fefferman, *op. cit.* (n. 39), pp. 97–98.
[42] U.S. Congress, Senate Subcommittee on Executive Reorganization of the Committee on Government Operations, *Hearings, Federal Role in Urban Affairs*, 89th Cong., 2nd Sess. (1966), Appendix to Part 1, p. 59.

The Housing Act of 1954 and subsequent acts have thus moved urban renewal from a program whose primary purpose was to improve housing for poor people towards a program whose purpose is more to renew the central city tax base and to recall middle and high-income whites from the suburbs to the city. HUD itself supports this interpretation. In the same Hearings before the Ribicoff Committee just quoted, the HUD presentation observes, "In effect the Congress has broadened urban renewal goals to the point where it is fruitless to attempt to distinguish whether non-residential renewal is now a primary, or still a secondary, goal of the program." [43]

In addition to the substantive changes made by the Housing Act of 1954, Congress in that Act made a procedural change. Communities were required to submit and have approved a Workable Program for Community Improvement before they could receive Title I funds. This Workable Program consisted of:

(a) Codes and ordinances establishing adequate standards of health and safety for a community's housing.
(b) A comprehensive plan for the community's future development.
(c) Analyses of the neighborhoods in the community to identify those where something should be done about blight.
(d) Administrative organization capable of coordinating and carrying out a community program.
(e) Financial resources to support the localities' share of an urban renewal program.
(f) Housing resources to meet the needs of those displaced by urban renewal.
(g) Assurance that the community as a whole is fully informed and has the fullest opportunity to take part in developing and executing an urban renewal program. [44]

Secretary Robert Weaver himself pointed out that the Workable Program has not been vigorously enforced. Of particular interest here to lower-income families, particularly in view of the emphasis

[43] *Ibid.*, p. 59.
[44] Robert Weaver, *The Urban Complex* (New York: Doubleday and Company, 1960), p. 85.

on participation in the War on Poverty, is the last condition, relating to community participation in developing and carrying out the renewal program. More than any of the other provisions of the program, this one has been honored more in the breach than in the observance. Most attempts at citizen participation have been mere ritual approval of plans presented to the citizens. Furthermore, Workable Program citizen committees historically have had very few low-income members. Citizen involvement by the poor has often been ad hoc organized opposition to the whole renewal venture—and thus has not been very welcome by cities committed to renewal.[45]

Since 1954 some efforts have been made to deal with the relocation grievances of the poor. The main emphasis has been on encouraging rehabilitation of dwellings in renewal areas so that the poor will not have to be displaced. Thus, in 1964 Congress passed a program providing, for the first time, direct federal low-interest rate (3%) loans. The loans were to go to property owners or long-term tenants in renewal areas for rehabilitation efforts necessary to make the property conform to the local housing code. The same year a provision permitting urban renewal capital grant funds for enforcing housing codes in urban renewal areas was put into the Act. Finally, in 1965, limited rehabilitation grants were authorized to low-income homeowners in urban renewal areas. Despite these attempts to meet the problem, HUD admits, "the aggregate volume of rehabilitated housing attained in these various programs . . . is modest compared with the tremendous need."[46]

Nonetheless, in the past few years, HUD has put major emphasis

[45] For a more thorough discussion of citizen participation, see James Q. Wilson, "Planning and Politics: Citizen Participation in Urban Renewal," Bellush and Hausknecht, op. cit. (n. 1), pp. 287–301.

It should also be noted that HUD has recently moved to foster more relevant citizen participation. Project Advisory Committees composed of residents are now required in urban renewal programs and in the new (1968) Neighborhood Development Programs. The purpose of the PAC's is "to participate in all decisions regarding the timing and location of all activities within the urban renewal area."

[46] U.S. Congress, Senate Subcommittee on Executive Reorganization, Committee on Government Operations, op. cit. (n. 42), p. 65.

on rehabilitation and code enforcement as a means of solving the housing problems of the poor. There are several problems with such an approach. If the market is tight, code enforcement, to be a realistic force, must be accompanied by rehabilitation (at rents the poor can afford) or by an additional supply of low-income housing elsewhere; otherwise the result will be a decreased supply of housing for low-income people—and it is difficult to see how that will improve anything.

Unfortunately, efforts at rehabilitation have invariably resulted in significant rent increases. Unless other low-income housing at pre-rehabilitation prices is readily available, the poor may quite unwillingly have to absorb these increases even though some may have preferred inferior housing at lower costs. Under these circumstances, rehabilitation does not seem feasible without accompanying rent supplements or rent control or both, unless, that is, the cost of rehabilitation can be significantly reduced. Towards this end there has recently been much discussion of the need for technological breakthroughs which would lower rehabilitation costs and, also, for a subsequent mass rehabilitation industry.

Urban renewal has, during the last decade, lost many of its liberal supporters because of its seeming nonconcern with problems of low-income families. HUD does, however, seem increasingly aware of the need for urban renewal to address itself more boldly to the problems of this group. In June, 1967, Secretary Weaver issued a set of priorities by which urban renewal applications could be judged. Top priority was given to applications which "contribute effectively to the conservation and expansion of housing for low and moderate income families; the development of employment opportunities and the renewal of areas with critical and urgent needs." [47]

Model cities legislation, passed in 1966, is, in many ways, simply an encouragement of this trend in urban renewal. The basic thrust of the legislation was to coordinate the city's fight on slums and blight and to allow for innovation in doing so. Cities were to sub-

[47] *HUD News*, No. 2651, June 2, 1967.

mit plans which dealt comprehensively with an entire neighbor-hood.[48] These plans consisted of series of federal programs already on the books, plus new and innovative programs drawn up by the cities themselves. These latter programs were to be financed partly by the federal government through a formula which gave the cities up to 80 percent of the local share of the federal grant-in-aid pro-grams included in their model cities plan. The Act specifically calls for "a substantial increase in the supply of housing of low and moderate cost." HUD, in its Senate testimony, specifically sug-gested this be done through a concentrated rehabilitation effort financed in part by the 80 percent supplemental grant. Since funds were limited (the program was sold as a demonstration), competi-tion among applicants for grants was high.

The most original contribution of model cities is the supplemen-tal grant. Cities have complained for years that they have suffered under the oppressive hand of the "Feds"; now they are given a chance to develop their own programs tailored to their own prob-lems. They have not been given much money with which to do this, however. In order to maximize the supplemental grant it is likely that cities will turn to the federal program where there is the most readily available supply of grant-in-aid matching fund money—urban renewal.

### Housing and the Political System: Housing Subsidies for Low-Income Families

In 1961 Congress passed, with much fanfare, a below-market-in-terest rental housing program, popularly known as "221 (d) (3)." The program is aimed primarily at the lower-middle income

[48] The legislation requires that a Model Cities Program provide for wide-spread citizen participation in the program. According to HUD guidelines, "Cities must work closely with neighborhood residents in all phases of the for-mulation of the plan as well as its execution. The process of involving resi-dents in decision-making during planning and program implementation should result in a plan and program that is responsive to their needs and recognizes and develops their competence as individuals and citizens." "Citizen Participa-tion," CDA Letter No. 1, pp. 2–3.

groups whose income was too high to qualify for public housing. Below-the-market-rate 100 percent loans established at 3 percent in 1965, are authorized to nonprofit organizations, cooperatives, and limited dividend corporations for construction or rehabilitation of five-family or larger rental dwellings. The below-market interest rate is subsidized by special assistance funds from FNMA (Federal National Mortgage Association; changed to GNMA—Government National Mortgage Association—in 1969).[49] Maximum income levels are usually several thousand dollars above those established for public housing.

The major importance of 221 (d) (3) as far as low-income families are concerned (it has not generated enough units to have had a significant filtration effect) is that the (d) (3) program has served as the vehicle for the rent-supplement program passed in 1965. In the rent-supplement program the federal government pays the difference between rent on an apartment in a rent-supplement project and 25 percent of the tenant's income. Rent-supplement projects must be approved by FHA and sponsors must sign a Regulatory Agreement requiring the landlord to clear his rents with the government. This provision prevents landlords from charging outrageous rents which would be borne by the government in the form of the rent supplement.

As in 221 (d) (3) housing, sponsors of rent-supplement projects must be either private nonprofit organizations, limited-dividend corporations, or cooperatives. Projects must pay the market-interest rate; the loan-to-value ratio, however, is the same as in the below-market interest rate 221 (d) (3) program (up to 100 percent for nonprofit sponsors).

Rent supplements, in its inception, was aimed at the group whose income was too high for public housing, in fact, the same group which benefits from 221 (d) (3). Indeed, in his 1965 message,

[49] FNMA special assistance programs guaranteed that originators of first mortgages would be able to sell their market-interest-rate mortgages to FNMA, which then charged the holder an interest rate substantially below the original market rate. FNMA obtained its funds by borrowing from the Treasury with authorization ceilings set by Congress.

the President stated that rent supplements was being groomed by the Administration to replace the 221 (d) (3) below-market program, which the Administration considered too great a drain on the Treasury. However, Congress changed the program so that it served only low-income people. Income limits on participants, identical with those in public housing, were placed in the legislation, as was a $2,000 limit on assets ($5,000 for the elderly). In addition, tenants had to be in one of the following categories:

1. displaced by governmental action
2. at least 62 years of age
3. physically handicapped
4. living in substandard housing
5. occupying living units destroyed or extensively damaged by natural disaster.[50]

For the tenant, under rent supplements, there are advantages claimed over public housing. The tenant is not required to move should his income rise above the maximum limit as he was until recently in public housing; rather his rent supplement will stop and he will assume the full rent payment himself. Again, unlike public housing, the tenant will not deal directly with the government at all, but with the private landlord who receives the supplement directly from the government and who determines who may be accepted into the project. In short, the landlord-tenant relationship is supposed to be no different from the traditional private relationship. The landlord may accept a significant percentage of tenants who will pay the full rent themselves. The stigma of institutionalized public housing will thus be avoided; at the same time the cost to the government will be less since it will not be involved in project management.

The most obvious difficulty with the rent-supplement program thus far is that it has not been adequately funded. One of the reasons it has not been adequately funded is the potential for foster-

[50] This section on rent supplements is drawn nearly wholly from Robert Ellickson's excellent account, *op. cit.* (n.26).

ing integration which some Congressmen have found in the program. Because there originally was no control by a local public agency as there is in public housing, rent-supplement projects could be located anywhere—perhaps even in suburbs where increasingly employment opportunities are to be found. Indeed, the first paragraph of preliminary FHA guidelines on rent supplements, issued in September, 1965, stated: "Important criteria with regard to approval of a rent supplement project will include full consideration of its contribution to assisting in integrating income groups and furthering the legal requirement and objectives of equal opportunity in housing." [51]

This statement received widespread publicity and resulted in quick withdrawal by FHA of the preliminary guidelines, when it appeared they might jeopardize appropriations for the supplement program. Despite the quick withdrawal, the Appropriations Committee added a local control rider to the appropriations. Indeed, in the context of an economy-minded Congress, the specter of integration has made rent supplements one of the prime targets for those bent on budget-cutting.

A more basic long-range difficulty with rent supplements (and 221 (d) (3) in general) is the limitations of the sponsoring nonprofit corporations. They are limited both in numbers and, perhaps more importantly, in knowledge—both in terms of financial know-how and project management. Efforts are being made by private groups to educate and help along interested sponsors. Recently 221 (d) (3) completions have accelerated. Over 100,000 had been completed by the end of 1969. However, due to its immediate impact on the federal budget (the entire cost of the mortgage is registered on the budget the year it is purchased), the program is being phased out in favor of Section 235.

Several proposals in 1967 focused upon homeownership subsidy for low-income people. Although there were a variety of such pro-

---

[51] "Rent Supplement Program Package," Federal Housing Administration MF Letter No. 63, September 28, 1965.

posals, they all basically depended upon the mechanism of a below-market interest rate subsidy administered either directly
through FHA or indirectly through a nonprofit corporation capitalized originally by the federal government. Such proposals at least
had the virtue of meeting the desires of the American public. Surveys have shown that the vast majority of Americans would prefer
to own their own homes.[52] In addition, George Sternlieb's study of
Newark points out quite clearly the importance of a proprietary interest in encouraging adequate maintenance.[53]

Secretary Weaver, on the other hand, questioned the desirability
of encouraging the very poor to own their homes. Not only would
such ownership burden them heavily with debt, he suggested, but
it would severely limit their mobility, which may be an important
factor in terms of improving employment situations. It should be
noted, however, that the proposed home-ownership plans were to
serve families with an income range of $4,000–$7,000, ignoring the
needs of those with the lowest income.[54]

A final approach suggested by a few academic housing experts
urges some reduction on further uses of housing subsidies. Adherents of this approach argue that housing is not the crucial problem
at all so far as the poor are concerned; the crucial problem is lack
of income. Public policy thus should be aimed at income maintenance rather than assuring adequate housing per se. Once income
is sufficient, adequate housing will be easily obtainable. The only
excuse for concentrating on housing subsidies is that they are a
more politically feasible form of redistribution of wealth than other
alternative policies. However, if housing efforts do not redistribute
income as efficiently or quickly to the poor as other politically acceptable measures, or if housing efforts themselves are not politically acceptable, then housing must be subordinated to other efforts.

[52] Glazer, *op. cit.* (n. 14), p. 31.
[53] Sternlieb, *op. cit.* (n. 18), p. 176.
[54] Such a program based on interest subsidies was enacted into law by Congress in 1968 (Section 235). See *ibid.*, p. 73.

## Housing and the Political System: Segregation, Nondiscrimination, and Integration

Segregated markets per se are an important factor in hindering the amelioration of poor housing conditions for Negroes. Particularly when the inner-city housing market is tight, the presence of segregated housing markets in the suburbs deprives Negroes of needed opportunities for housing. In addition, in nearly all cities, jobs are increasingly migrating to the suburbs. The Negro, if he is to respond to this shifting opportunity structure in employment, must either make use of extremely poor mass transportation facilities going outwards from the central city or he must move to where the jobs are. The first choice does not seem a viable alternative; the real choice is for Negroes to move to the suburbs or to have their employment situation worsen.

Civil rights advocates have long complained that both FHA and VA have not approved loans to Negroes. Rather, these agencies have represented the biases of realtors and lending institutions with whom they work closely on the local level. In response to this, President Kennedy issued, in 1962, an Executive Order prohibiting discrimination in *new* housing provided with federal aid, including insurance of loans. In addition, discrimination in new or old housing owned by the federal government was outlawed. Although the Executive Order had a millennium ring about it when it was issued, the results have been consistent with what had occurred before. A study by the American Friends Service Committee concluded:

1. Executive Order 11063 is being widely and flagrantly violated by builders, brokers and lenders.
2. Implementation of the Order by the Federal Housing Administration (FHA) and Veterans Administration (VA) has been at best ineffective, and at worst subversive of the goal of equal opportunity in housing.[55]

[55] American Friends Service Committee, *A Report to the President on Equal Opportunity in Housing* (Philadelphia: American Friends Service Committee, May, 1967), p. 1.

FHA, after having undergone a series of harsh attacks in 1967, responded with several changes in guidelines designed to eliminate discrimination in handling of FHA loans. Then, in 1968, Congressional passage of a fair-housing law made nondiscrimination the law of the land. However, most of the Northern industrial states (and a scattering of others) already had state fair-housing laws. Their success has not been spectacular. Enforcement procedures are usually cumbersome and require extraordinary activity on the part of the aggrieved. Furthermore, they have not been accompanied by concerted efforts to educate Negroes who might desire to move about the opportunities that do exist, or about how to take advantage of these opportunities.

The whole question of the desirability of integration as a short-range goal has recently come under scrutiny. Some, including black militants, have argued that immediate priority ought to be given to improving the quality of life in the ghetto, which is where most low-income Negroes will be for years to come. And, at any rate, few Negroes wish to move out into predominantly white neighborhoods and less than a majority prefer mixed neighborhoods. Based on a sample of Negroes in several large cities, Gary T. Marx found the following distribution: [56]

Type of neighborhood preferred if all equally well kept up:

| | |
|---|---|
| Mostly Negroes | 62% |
| Mixed or no difference | 31 |
| Mostly white | 4 |
| Don't know | 3 |

Government response to this switch of emphasis by groups representing the Negro community is, at the time of this writing, still somewhat uncertain. The response of the housing decision-making elite to this question, as well as to others concerning housing policy is discussed in Chapter 8.

[56] Gary T. Marx, *Protest and Prejudice: A Study of Belief in the Black Community* (New York: Harper and Row, 1967), p. 176.

# CHAPTER 3

# The Housing Policy System

## Introductory Note

The findings presented in the following five chapters represent a first attempt to describe and generalize about the way policy is made within the national housing political system. As such, they ought to be viewed as exploratory and suggestive rather than as proven assertions. It is exceedingly tempting for political scientists, in describing the public policy process, to impose more order on it than such a system actually possesses, for classification and generalization are the goals of all social scientists. James MacGregor Burns has written:

After spending three years in the White House Office under Kennedy, Arthur Schlesinger, Jr., concluded that "the historian tends in retrospect to make the processes of decision far more tidy and rational than they are: to assume that people have fixed positions and represent fixed interests and to impose a pattern on what is actually a swirl if not a chaos. I think the historian doesn't realize the opaqueness of the process." The political scientist, who shares the temptation to inflict patterns on disorderly political processes, may also underestimate the almost anarchic nature of decision-making among a group of men without established relationships meeting perhaps in a crisis amidst a stream of murky information in order to grapple with the shifting activities and plans of rival politicians or foreign leaders.[1]

[1] James MacGregor Burns, *Presidential Government* (Boston: Houghton Mifflin Company, 1966), p. 143.

However, the fact that order is not easily imposed on such a system does not mean that order does not exist. Rather it testifies to the exploratory nature of the study. What is at first random and inexplicable may yield to generalization easily after more intensive study.

The primary data from these chapters were derived from approximately sixty wide-ranging and unstructured interviews with active participants, representing a variety of perspectives within the housing policy process. In order to conduct these interviews in such a way so that honest and frank responses were encouraged, it was necessary to guarantee anonymity to each respondent before the interview. For this reason, no citations will be given from these interviews. Secondary data, particularly for the first sections in Chapter 4, were drawn from existing literature on housing and housing economics.

## The Nongovernmental Environment

The federal housing decision-making system is only a part of a much larger system which allocates values (nonauthoritative) in the area of housing. Most values in this larger housing system are allocated by the private market or through other nonfederal institutions. It follows from this that the federal housing decision-making system, the focus of this study, can neither be comprehended nor appreciated without taking into account the environment in which it operates. This environment (the wider systems) both defines the problem and sets the constraints within which decisions are made.[2]

These constraints, presently, must be assumed to be given so far as those within the federal housing system are concerned, although

[2] "System theory dictates a strategy of research which is in basic opposition to reductionism or the immediate pushing to some more elementary level for an understanding of social-psychological phenomena. The first step should always be to go to the next higher level of system organization to study the dependence of the system in question upon the supersystem of which it is a part, for the supersystem sets the limits of variance of behavior of the dependent

some constraints would be, in principle, open to manipulation by the federal housing elite if such manipulation were politically feasible. The most important set of constraints concerns the private economy, and more particularly, the private housing industry, as these affect the supply of low-income housing. Let us assume, for convenience, that the goal of government housing policy is as expressed in the Housing Act of 1949, to assure adequate housing for all Americans who are not able to obtain it on the private market. As has already been pointed out, most low-income families obtain accommodations through the filtering process by which more affluent families move to new housing, setting up a chain reaction of upward mobility which ultimately opens up more housing to low-income groups.[3]

The gap which the government must then bridge to provide adequate housing for all people varies according to the performance in the private housing market itself, both in terms of new starts and vacancy rates in the existing stock. In years in which the homebuilding industry has low numbers of housing starts, the housing problems of low-income people are exacerbated, thus increasing the scope of the problem so far as government is concerned. Anthony Downs, a noted real estate analyst, and political scientist, explains why:

Unless there is a general expansion in the supply of housing offered on the market at a relatively rapid rate, housing conditions for slum dwellers cannot improve . . . high levels of annual housing starts will create a "loose" housing market in general by providing more new units than there are new households formed. Only if such "looseness" prevails can there be an improvement in the housing conditions at the bottom of the inventory. This is true even though persons living in bottom-of-the-inventory units cannot afford new housing. They do not even efficiently

system. More analytic study can then explore the contributions of subsystems to this limited range of variance. For example, if we want to study patterns of cooperation and conflict within an industrial company, our first step would not be to look at the informal standards in work groups but to study the position of the company in the industry as a whole." Daniel Katz and Robert Kahn, *The Social Psychology of Organizations* (New York: John Wiley, 1966), p. 58.

[3] See Chap. 2, p. 23.

gain the benefits of the trickle-down (filtering) process. Yet that process works with amazing efficiency in transmitting low vacancy rates and rising rents downward through the housing stock. As a result, in periods when housing starts are cut back but general prosperity remains strong, housing conditions immediately worsen in the ghetto. Vacancies decline, rents rise, and landlords reduce maintenance as they realize their competition is declining.[4]

The number of housing starts depends in large part on the availability of mortgage money at reasonable terms. Unfortunately, the availability of funds and interest rates is determined with little reference to the needs of housing. Thus, the Vietnam War undoubtedly acted as a major constraint on private construction. It resulted in huge federal expenditures for the war effort with consequent federal borrowing to finance those expenditures. The government, thus, by increasing the demand for loanable funds, drove up the interest rate. A high rate of investment by business—encouraged by a 7 percent investment credit—further contributed to the soaring interest rate. This upward trend in interest rates was reinforced by the reliance on monetary rather than fiscal policy to dampen the consequent inflationary pressures in the economy.

Housing in general (including government programs which work through the private mortgage market) suffers when interest rates rise. Since mortgage-lending institutions' rates to depositors are slow to change, prospective depositors will divert their funds to government bonds and other financial intermediaries. As a result, the amount of loanable funds of the mortgage-lending institutions, particularly savings and loan associations, will fall as interest rates rise. The consequence of all this is greatly to limit decision-makers within the federal housing policy system unless they are willing to think in terms of developing new and better credit institutions for the housing industry which would somehow divorce sources of funds and housing interest rates from those of the rest of the economy. This is not an easy thing to do.

[4] U.S. Congress, Senate Subcommittee on Executive Reorganization of the Committee on Government Operations, *Hearings, Federal Role in Urban Affairs*, 90th Cong., 1st Sess.(1967), Part 17, pp. 3495–96.

Another clear constraint on the supply side concerns the scarcity of equity capital in the housing market. Investors of equity in both private and governmental programs compare prospective returns on their investments in housing to alternative investments elsewhere in the economy. Again the attractiveness of other investments is something housing policy-makers can only react to but cannot control, except as those investments affect the relative attractiveness of housing. Without some form of government subsidy to the investor, the low return on investment for new low-income rental housing acts as a nearly insurmountable barrier. The mortgage subsidy provision in Sections 235 and 236 of the 1968 Housing Act is an attempt to deal with this problem.

It has been disputed whether present low-income programs offer insufficient subsidies to attract equity capital or whether some other factor, such as inadequate appropriations or excessive government red tape, is a more important cause for restricting the supply of housing for low-income people. The lack of attractive incentives for equity capital formed the basis of both Senators Percy's (R–Ill.) and Robert Kennedy's (D–N.Y.) respective housing bills in the Ninetieth Congress.

Also on the supply side, there are cost factors which both drive up the price of housing and cut into the profit margin of builders, thus cutting relative attractiveness. Primary among these is the cost of land, which has doubled over the last two decades.[5] Again, there is virtually no way for housing policy-makers to react to this unless they begin to think in terms of controlling land prices, either through land subsidy, write-down, advance land acquisition, or land taxation. Outmoded building codes also contribute substantially to cost and, again, because those codes are locally regulated, have been beyond the purview of the Federal housing establishment. The relative cost of both labor and materials in the construction of a building, on the other hand, has decreased, but there is bitter debate within the industry concerning the pace of further cost-reducing innovation. Homebuilders accuse the

[5] *Ibid.*, p. 3509.

craft guilds involved in the construction process, particularly the building trades unions, of opposing innovation, both in terms of efficiency and new materials. Labor, for its part, accuses the builders of attempting to lower standards through new industrial prefab techniques.[6]

On the demand side, the problem set by the environment is much clearer. The market for new housing is almost entirely a middle- and upper-income suburban one because the suburbs are usually the only area with land available. As a major durable good, housing demands are likely to reflect quickly any major trend in the economy quite emphatically; thus, housing demand is likely to fall as uncertainty sets in. Since most low-income people are ultimately housed through the vagaries of the filtering process, the extent of housing demand among middle and upper-income groups determines, to a large extent, their own housing situation.

Because low-income people have insufficient income to compete in the private market, it has been suggested that the most effective approach to housing problems would be to raise their income (or supplement it for housing purposes), thus providing a demand for the housing industry to respond to. However, it is not known to what extent this increased demand would indeed result in increased supply and to what extent it would merely result in price increases in present units, both homes and apartments. The real questions are how much demand would have to increase at the lower-income level before supply increased significantly and how much prices would rise in the interim. Again, this limits the options open to the federal housing system unless that system's elite is willing to control rents and prices, or set them, as in effect they do, in the rent-supplement program.[7]

Federal efforts are further limited by a set of constraints at the

[6] President Johnson's Committee on Urban Housing made recommendations to come to grips with problems on the supply side.

[7] For further discussion of the economic constraints on federal housing policy, see Martin Meyerson, Barbara Terrett, and William L. C. Wheaton, *Housing People and Cities* (New York: McGraw-Hill, 1962), pp. 2–9; and Sherman J. Maisel, *Financing Real Estate* (New York: McGraw-Hill, 1965).

community level, for nearly all federal housing programs affecting low-income people are dependent upon local initiative. The most important of these constraints is local opposition to Negroes in general, and to integration in particular. Such opposition makes it extremely difficult for local governments to approve public housing, rent-supplement, or 221 (d) (3) programs, or to agree upon sites for construction. At the same time there still exists a general ideological opposition to federal housing programs, although this seems to be lessening. The only option open here to the housing policy system is for the federal government to assume the initiative in housing from the local level, and the political barriers to this step are so obvious that it is not even contemplated as a possibility.

## The Federal Government as Environment

The federal housing system is also a subsystem of the larger federal government decision-making system. Since federal resources are scarce, the share going to housing depends, in part, on competing demands for those resources within the federal budget. The existence of the war in Vietnam, for example, placed a major strain on the federal budget and greatly limited resources available to other domestic programs during the mid- and late 1960's. Resources open for allocation in the budget to domestic programs are further limited by the relatively high proportion of nonmanipulable expenditures in the budget (agricultural support programs, veteran's pensions, aid to dependent children, etc.). Housing competes for the remaining available resources with other nonfixed domestic needs.

The Administration's acceptance of the New Economics as a legitimate means to manipulate the economy further limited the options open to the federal housing system. The threat of inflation due to excess aggregate demand (again a problem greatly aggravated by the Vietnam War) specified, according to the New Economics, government reaction to restrict the economic expansion.

Ideally, fiscal policy would have played a major role in a balanced policy, but that route was closed because of Congressional opposition. It was, therefore, necessary to rely during the period under discussion almost entirely on monetary policy as influenced by upward movements in the discount rate of the Federal Reserve Board. The intended result of this policy was to dampen the economy through higher interest rates. Unfortunately, a secondary result was adversely to affect housing construction, which is the sector of the economy most sensitive to changing rates. Not surprisingly, therefore, the housing industry was the most vigorous supporter of President Johnson's 10 percent tax surcharge.

As a further largely psychological effort to cut aggregate demand, the President can hold back on the expenditure of already appropriated funds, as he did during early 1967 with FNMA special assistance funds, again adversely affecting federal housing programs for a nonhousing reason.

### Environmental Demands

The environment does more than place limits on a system. It also provides inputs (demands) to which the system reacts. Objectively the need for improved housing for low-income people has existed for many years. But, until the mid-1960's this need was, to a large extent, not translated into a sustained demand on the political system. It is true that groups such as labor and the National Housing conference pushed with varying intensity, low-income housing legislation. However, they did so in the traditional terms of seeking an increased amount of public housing, a demand which ran into extremely strong opposition from other elements in the federal housing system and its environment. In addition, the housing problems they had in mind during most of the period from 1935–60 were primarily those of low-income but employed whites, particularly those in labor unions.

Few organized groups pressed effectively for action on the housing problems of low-income Negroes, a significant number of whom were unemployed. The problem of low-income housing for either racial group received little support from important opinion leaders, the mass media, and the mass public. As a result, therefore, of the strong opposition to public housing and the general lack of concern about low-income housing as an urgent problem, low-income housing was not granted a top priority either within the federal government generally or within the federal housing system more specifically. During most of the postwar era, the major demands on this system emanated from the housing industry and middle-class Americans to finance the movement of the white urban middle class to the suburbs. This was done through the FHA mortgage programs and the savings and loan industry supported by the Federal Home Loan Bank Board.

However, as the preceding discussion has indicated, the federal housing system is not isolated from social and political trends occurring in the nonhousing sectors. Rather, it is closely tied to broad social forces. Thus, it was the Negro revolution of the early and mid-1960's which brought poor housing, as well as other problems of low-income Negroes, to the level of visibility and which led to demands on the political system for action. The riots of 1964–68 reinforced this trend and focused attention on housing needs, since poor housing is probably the most visible deprivation suffered by low-income groups.

These events led to new demands, including the direct improvement of housing conditions of the poor. This housing demand entered the national political system through the activity of largely white, liberal groups sympathetic to the problems of the Negro poor as well as through elected politicians either directly representing low-income Negroes or sympathetic to their plight. In many cases these groups or individuals may have been transferring the demands of Negro organizations or groups with whom they had contact at local levels. In addition, other groups—in some cases very powerful and significant ones—whose self-interest coincided with better housing for low-income Negroes, added their voices. The National Association of Home Builders was probably the most significant of these. Most Negro organizations, however, remained inactive nationally.

The inputs were increased in effectiveness by demands from a portion of the public (and many decision-makers) to respond to the riots by eliminating some of the grievances which caused them—the most visible of which was poor housing. In effect, this was a demand transmitted to nearly all elements in the government to return the social system to equilibrium—that is, to assure stability. Other contrary demands entered the system calling for the use of as much force as necessary to put down riots and urging that rioters not be "rewarded" for their criminal activity.

A much more diffuse demand may have been in the end, however, most important. The housing elite gradually responded to the concern other elements of society were expressing towards the problems of poverty. Opinion leaders in America and the mass media began to focus on the poor, particularly as the civil rights revolution gave way to its more militant phase. Probably partially in response to this, and partially in response to his own intellectual and emotional predilections, President Johnson made the "War on Poverty" the keystone of his legislative efforts and the major domestic issue in his 1964 campaign. The Office of Economic Opportunity (OEO) and its activities undoubtedly acted as a spur on HUD to pay more attention to the problems of the poor. Later, public commissions, such as the Kerner Commission on urban disorders, focused directly on problems of ghetto dwellers. So did the Ribicoff hearings in 1966–67. Both of these received wide publicity in the communications media.

The result was that, in broad terms, housing problems began to redefine themselves in terms of the poor, and the Negro ghetto poor in particular. Partly, no doubt, they redefined themselves because real problems were created for decision-makers. Noise and confusion rather than orderly group demands were effective as demands because they threatened the stability of the housing system and called forth an equilibrating response. Thus, Negro groups threatened to thwart urban renewal programs in many cities. Their demands had to be dealt with. But it also seems clear that the housing elite itself changed—partly through replacement of members—its own personal attitudes and sense of priorities in accordance with major events in the rest of society.

## Organized Groups in the Environment

Operating in the environment of the housing policy process are a variety of organized interest groups.[8] Much of the activity of these groups is directed towards what David Truman refers to as "the attempt to achieve effective access to points of decision."[9] Not all of these groups do obtain access—the establishment of communication channels with members of the decision-making elite. Nor is access, once obtained, necessarily effective, since decision-makers can listen without either heeding or agreeing. For this study, the groups selected for examination included all those which put forth a major effort to influence housing policy and, in addition, a variety of lesser groups selected so that viewpoints not represented by the major more active groups might also be considered.

✓The National Association of Housing and Redevelopment Officials (NAHRO) is a professional organization for members and employees of local public housing agencies and renewal agencies. Although not a lobby, because of its tax-exempt status, NAHRO has long been one of the most visible forces behind "liberal" legislation. Its *main* interest is urban renewal and public housing, and its main thrust is to push for more and more of each. It also is a strong supporter of model cities. NAHRO has been somewhat suspicious of innovations which threaten to work outside the traditional framework of local public housing agencies. Thus, for example, it was a vigorous opponent of the rent-supplement program in

---

[8] In some cases, organized groups, or parts of them, may be considered as a part of the conversion process rather than merely a part in the environment. This phenomenon shall be referred to later.

[9] David Truman, *The Governmental Process* (New York: Alfred A. Knopf, 1951), p. 264.

1965, and some of its members have given only nominal support since then. More recently NAHRO has begun to represent the need for effective metropolitan planning.

The National Housing Conference (NHC) is considered by many as the lobby arm of NAHRO. It consists of members from various "public interest organizations," as well as distinguished individuals who share NHC's goals of a long-term commitment to building housing for low- and moderate-income people. Traditionally it has been strongly identified with public housing and urban renewal. Whereas NAHRO is likely to concentrate on access to HUD, NHC aims its main efforts at the Hill.

The AFL-CIO at the national level has been a strong supporter of almost all housing programs for low- and moderate-income people. It is viewed by many as the most effective lobby at the Congressional stage, mostly because of its ready access to those Congressmen whose constituency includes significant elements of organized labor. Because it is not a housing "expert," labor's role is usually, though not exclusively, one of rounding up support for programs proposed by others. Both labor and NHC have historically sought volume for established programs far beyond what the Administration has been willing to recommend or the Congress ready to grant. The Industrial Union Division of the AFL-CIO, which disappeared when the UAW withdrew from that organization, was especially active in lobbying for housing on city-oriented programs and tended to be somewhat more liberal than the rest of the AFL-CIO.

The United States Conference of Mayors is an organization consisting of mayors of the larger cities. It supports programs which make available to cities as much money as possible with as few strings as possible attached. Its major effort is thus aimed not at drawing up specific programs, but at bringing *money* to cities. The Conference is, according to several respondents, an organization dominated by Chicago's Mayor Daley; its Executive Director, John Gunther, has been quite close to higher members of the institutionalized Presidency (see p. 81). In addition to the Conference's influence at this level, its members can achieve publicity for its desires quite easily. For the same reason, its members often are effective lobbyists with key Congressmen whose constituencies lie within the borders of their city. The National League of Cities (NLC) is a similar organization except that its membership includes mayors of all cities regardless of size. It works quite closely with the Conference of Mayors.

✓The National Association of Home Builders (NAHB), in the 1960's, was the major housing industry organization to throw its support behind Administration programs to house low- and moderate-income people. Consisting mostly of small builders, the Association historically had opposed government programs. As late as the 1950's it attacked public housing as "socialistic and communistic." However, in the sixties NAHB grew more pragmatic. It now favors nearly any program which will mean more houses for its members to construct. Thus, the emphasis on housing for low- and moderate-income people has been favorably perceived as opening up a whole new market to the builders. It also is in the forefront of the fight in opposition to high interest rates, since high interest rates usually dry up the supply of money necessary to finance homebuilding.

The major financial institutions connected with the housing industry are the Mortgage Bankers Association (MBA), the American Bankers Association (ABA), the U.S. Savings and Loan Association (USS & LA), and the National Association of Mutual Savings Banks. Since all of these deal with housing mortgages, their major concern is that government programs do not interfere adversely with the normal operations of the mortgage market. Thus, they oppose direct government loans and subsidized interest-rate programs which operate outside the normal mortgage market. However, both the MBA and the Mutual Savings Banks Association supported the rent-supplement program since it works through the mortgage market. All the above financial organizations also supported legislation to free the FHA interest rate ceiling to make FHA-insured mortgages competitive with other investments during periods of rising interest rates. The maximum FHA mortgage rate was pushed upwards twice during 1968–69. The Mutual Savings Bank, and to a lesser extent the MBA, actively attempt to influence broad social programs, while the ABA and USS & LA concentrate their energies on more technical matters of great interest to them. In more general terms, the financial organizations, with the exception of the Mutual Savings Banks Association, which is more progressive, are likely to react in a somewhat cautious and skeptical manner to efforts to house low- and moderate-income people whom these organizations have traditionally viewed as poor risks. For this reason, the Mortgage Bankers Association opposed using the FHA programs as a means of improving social conditions of the poor.

The National Association of Real Estate Boards (NAREB) is an organization composed of the nation's realtors. More than any other organization NAREB has the reputation of supporting what could loosely be called the conservative viewpoint in housing matters. It has been the spearhead of opposition to open housing laws —whether federal, state, or local. In addition, it still opposes public housing as well as subsidized interest-rate programs. Despite opposition during 1965, NAREB switched to support of the rent supplement when they began to perceive it as an alternative to public housing. Although NAREB put a substantial amount of effort into lobbying, many respondents suggested that its rather consistent stance in opposition renders it relatively ineffective at influencing policy.

The National Association for the Advancement of Colored People (NAACP) is a mass membership organization which espouses a moderate civil rights viewpoint. Its major effort in housing has been directed at obtaining open-housing laws, and its lobbyist, Clarence Mitchell, is given major credit for obtaining passage of the open-housing law in 1968.[10] However, in other areas of housing policy, the NAACP was practically moribund from 1964 to

[10] "Civil Rights Lobbying," *Congressional Quarterly*, April 26, 1968, p. 931.

1968. It had no staff expert on housing nor any particular position on most housing matters other than nondiscrimination.

The National Committee against Discrimination in Housing (NCDH) is a small organization whose major interest is to open up the suburbs to all races. It has specialized in research directed towards HUD and more broadly at the educated public in its attempts to bring about policy change. NCDH's pamphlet *How the Federal Government Builds Ghettos* [11] has received fairly wide publicity. NCDH has consistently criticized HUD for discrimination by local offices in granting of FHA loans to Negroes. It has also attacked urban renewal as "Negro removal," claiming that, in aggregate, urban renewal has destroyed more housing for low-income Negroes through clearance than it has produced. [12]

The Urban League also has concentrated on achieving nondiscrimination in housing. However, primarily due to its Executive Director, Whitney Young, the League has taken a more active interest in other aspects of housing policy than the NAACP. Young has pushed for an expanded supply of housing for minority groups. He has particularly favored programs to involve private capital in low-income housing, such as 221 (d) (3) and rent supplements. As a tax-exempt organization the League is strictly prohibited from lobbying before Congress.

The Congress of Racial Equality (CORE) and its Student Non-Violent Coordinating Committee (SNCC) generally support the position that efforts should be put into improving housing conditions within the ghetto rather than integrating the suburbs. Although SNCC has been relatively quiet on housing, CORE has called for a massive federal effort to expand housing supply for low-income people and to improve the present supply. The organization has strongly supported a comprehensive program similar to the one sponsored by Senator Robert Kennedy in Bedford-Stuyvesant, which features a corporation with the poor represented on the

[11] National Committee against Discrimination in Housing, *How the Federal Government Builds Ghettos* (New York: NCDH, 1967).
[12] *Ibid.*, p. 7.

board of directors. The corporation is planned, not only to finance housing for the poor, but also to employ and train community workers to do the work. CORE also has attacked urban renewal as not responsive to the needs of black people.

The American Institute of Planners (AIP) is the professional organization of city planners. It has placed major emphasis on the need for comprehensive planning, relating housing to a host of other equally important variables such as employment, transportation, health, aesthetics, and others. It has particularly pushed New Town planning. Because it is a tax-exempt organization, however, it puts most of its efforts into affecting HUD guidelines rather than influencing legislation.

A recently organized group which involves itself in housing policy is the National Urban Coalition, an organization of mayors, labor leaders, and businessmen. The Coalition has put its weight behind efforts to improve housing conditions for low-income Negroes. It particularly has pushed programs which involve a partnership between government and the private sector, putting resources at the command of the private sector to work in solving problems of the ghetto. Thus, it has been very much in favor of programs such as rent supplement, 221 (d) (3), and turnkey public housing, although it also supports other government programs particularly 235 and 236.

## Access and Representation

In order to determine how much access each of these groups has to members of the decision-making elite, members of that elite were asked how often they communicated with each of the organizations over the course of a year. The question was closed, and the alternatives were "many times," "occasionally," and "almost never." The results are presented in Table 1.

The organizations with the best access ("many times" plus "occasionally") are those which were strong supporters of the housing policy of the Johnson Administration and of federal efforts to improve housing in general. In some cases, these organizations were

Table 1. Decision-Makers' Communication
with Organizations

| Organization | How often decision-makers communicated with organization | | | |
|---|---|---|---|---|
| | Many times | Occasionally | Almost never | No answer |
| Conference of Mayors | 22 | 22 | 12 | 12 |
| NAHB | 20 | 29 | 6 | 13 |
| National League of Cities | 19 | 21 | 16 | 12 |
| Urban Coalition | 14 | 11 | 19 | 24[a] |
| AFL–CIO | 13 | 27 | 15 | 13 |
| NHC | 13 | 27 | 15 | 13 |
| NAHRO | 13 | 26 | 16 | 13 |
| NAACP or Urban League[a] | 12 | 21 | 23 | 12 |
| MBA | 9 | 25 | 22 | 12 |
| NAREB | 7 | 19 | 29 | 13 |
| AIP | 6 | 16 | 35 | 11 |
| NCDH | 6 | 11 | 38 | 13 |
| ABA | 5 | 17 | 33 | 13 |
| USS & LA | 4 | 22 | 29 | 13 |
| Mutual Savings Banks | 3 | 9 | 21 | 35[a] |
| SNCC or CORE[b] | 2 | 12 | 41 | 13 |

[a] The Urban Coalition and National Association of Mutual Savings Banks were added to the list of organizations after nearly half of the interviews were completed, which accounts for the high percentage of no answers.
[b] The NAACP and Urban League were grouped together in the question, as were SNCC and CORE, because it was felt communication with either one of the pair would result in much the same views being represented.

somewhat ahead of Administration policy. In the middle are the more conservative financial and realtor groups, many of which are quite chary of federal efforts in the housing market. The groups with the least access are those advocating the most change—the planners and the militant Negro organizations.

However, mere communication does not necessarily imply that a group's views have entered into the decision-making process. It is *effective* access, not simply access for which groups strive. The question to be pursued, then, is whether a group's views are *represented* within the decision-making elite. Thus, in addition to being asked about frequency of communication, the members of the decision-making elite were also asked whether they usually agreed or disagreed with the views of each of the groups. The question was as follows: "Do you usually agree or disagree with their stand?: (1) very highly agree; (2) agree more than disagree; (3) disagree more than agree; (4) very highly disagree; and (5) usually do not know what position is."

When combined with answers to the question concerning frequency of communication, a useful typology of representation can be developed. First, however, it was necessary to collapse categories in each question. Thus, answers of "many times" and "occasionally" to the communication-frequency question were added together and put into one category called "much communication." At the same time, on the following question, the categories of "very highly agree" and "agree more than disagree" were collapsed to a category called "agree"; similarly, "very highly disagree" and "disagree" were added together and called "disagree."

The typology thus consists of a two-by-three table with six possible classifications. Much communication plus agreement is considered "representation"; almost no communication plus agreement is looked upon as "virtual representation." In the second case the organization's views are represented through members within the decision-making elite who hold similar views, even though the organization does not communicate—or has no access to—these members. Much communication plus disagreement is termed "pressure," whereas little communication plus disagreement appears to be a case of "mutual antagonism." Little communication plus lack of knowledge about views of an organization suggests "lack of effort" on the part of the organization, since access, at least on the level of formally presenting views to the elite, is relatively easy to achieve at nearly all levels of the housing policy system. Much communication plus lack of knowledge of an organization's position was viewed as evidence of that organization's "incompetence." The typology can thus be pictured (results follow in Table 2):

|  | *Much communication* | *Little communication* |
|---|---|---|
| *Agree* | Representation | Virtual representation |
| *Disagree* | Pressure | Mutual antagonism |
| *Do not know* | Incompetence | Lack of effort or interest |

Table 2. Organizational Influence

| *Organization* | *Representation* | *Virtual representation* | *Pressure* | *Mutual antagonism* | *Lack of effort* | *Incompetent* | *No answer* |
|---|---|---|---|---|---|---|---|
| Conference of Mayors | 37 | 3 | 2 | 0 | 3 | 0 | 23 |
| NHC | 33 | 5 | 0 | 0 | 5 | 1 | 14 |
| AFL–CIO | 33 | 5 | 0 | 2 | 2 | 0 | 26 |
| NLC | 33 | 5 | 1 | 2 | 3 | 0 | 24 |
| NAHRO | 30 | 4 | 2 | 2 | 2 | 2 | 26 |
| NAHB | 30 | 2 | 11 | 1 | 1 | 0 | 23 |
| NAACP or Urban League | 25 | 9 | 0 | 2 | 7 | 0 | 25 |
| Urban Coalition | 22 | 6 | 0 | 0 | 6 | 0 | 34 |
| MBA | 20 | 2 | 7 | 9 | 7 | 1 | 22 |
| AIP | 18 | 8 | 0 | 2 | 14 | 1 | 25 |
| USS & LA | 14 | 3 | 6 | 8 | 11 | 2 | 24 |
| NCDH | 13 | 8 | 1 | 4 | 13 | 1 | 28 |
| SNCC or CORE | 8 | 5 | 2 | 11 | 15 | 1 | 26 |
| Mutual Savings Banks | 7 | 3 | 3 | 2 | 9 | 1 | 43 |
| NAREB | 7 | 1 | 14 | 17 | 3 | 0 | 26 |
| ABA | 6 | 1 | 8 | 12 | 14 | 4 | 23 |

Again, it is the groups which in general terms supported the Johnson Administration programs which are the best represented. Moreover, it is the more conservative groups rather than the more radical groups whose views were most rejected by members of the elite. NAREB, probably the most conservative of the groups listed was classified as a "pressure" group by fourteen members of the decision-making elite, and as mutually antagonistic by seventeen more, making a grand total of thirty-one who disagreed with that organization's views. ABA with twenty, MBA with sixteen, and USS & LA with fourteen followed NAREB as organizations with whose views the most decision-makers were in disagreement.

The change groups (moderate and militant civil rights and Negro groups plus the planners) present the most interesting case. Critiques of group theory have suggested that "potential" groups with such attitudes either are not likely to become actual organized groups or to be allowed access to the decision-making elite.[13] The data, however, suggest that an additional—or perhaps alternative—major deterrent to effective representation of their views is simply lack of effort on the part of these organizations. Thus, of the four highest groups in the classification of lack of effort—meaning decision-makers did not know the group's views —three were change groups: SNCC or CORE with fifteen, AIP with fourteen, and NCDH with thirteen. The top three groups in the classification of virtual representation—little communication but agreement with views—were also change groups: NAACP or Urban League with nine, NCDH with eight, and AIP with eight. For various reasons, these groups apparently opt to put their efforts elsewhere.[14]

## The Low-Income Housing Policy System Conversion Process

The federal housing system (for redistributive decisions) consists itself of several separate subsystems. In the order in which they

[13] Grant McConnell, *Private Power and American Democracy* (New York: Alfred A. Knopf, 1967), p. 349.

[14] For an attempted explanation of this phenomenon, see Mancur Olson, *The Logic of Collective Action* (Cambridge, Mass.: Harvard University Press, 1965). See also Harold Wolman and Norman Thomas, "Negro Groups and Public Policy: The Cases of Housing and Education," to be published in *Journal of Politics*, 1970–71.

would occur in any particular redistributive policy decision they are: (1) the policy-formulation subsystem; (2) the substantive-legislation subsystem; (3) the appropriations subsystem; and (4) the operations subsystem. The subsystems (particularly one, two, and four) are overlapping to some extent in membership, but analytically each of them is distinct. Because they do overlap, various institutions may at the same time be involved in more than one subsystem. As a result an institution (or part of it) may constitute part of its own environment in a subsystem, even if it is a part of that subsystem.

The policy-formulation subsystem consists of three stages, although the order in which these stages occur is not invariable. New programs must be proposed or developed (ideas must be brought forward for change), the Administration must accept or reject these new programs, and it must place a priority on the political effort necessary to bring into being these new programs relative to other alternative expenditures of political energy.

Partly due to President Johnson's disenchantment with the inability of HHFA to propose imaginative new programs and partly because of Albert Rains' (D–Ala., Chairman of the Housing Subcommittee of the House Banking and Currency Committee) retirement in 1964, the government task force became a major focus for housing policy formulation. The task force combined with the White House staff, the Budget Bureau, and the highest officials at HUD in efforts to develop "Administration" housing policy during the Johnson era.

The substantive-legislative stage involves legislative drafting, Congressional committee consideration, lobbying, and Congressional passage (or nonpassage). Congressional committee consideration and Congressional passage are likely to be the most important so far as redistributive change is concerned.

The appropriations stage involves largely the same institutions associated with the institutionalized presidency as were active in the policy-formulation state (with the exception of the task force) and, in addition, Congressional appropriations subcommittees dealing with housing.

The operations stage is that part of the process in which guidelines and regulations are developed to implement programs authorized by Congress. HUD itself dominates this stage.

# CHAPTER 4

# Policy Formulation

## Environment

Policy is not formulated in a vacuum. Indeed, in many ways, what environmental factors prevent policy from being are more important than what policy actually is.[1] As has already been noted, a variety of economic, financial, and community restraints limit policy options open for the housing arena. In addition to these, actors engaged in the process of policy formulation within the housing policy system are constrained by important political and institutional factors.

The political mood of the country as translated in Congress probably comprises the most severe restraint. The Administration is loath to put its prestige on the line by presenting programs which are unlikely to generate significant support in Congress. Thus, despite the fact that large numbers of the Johnson Administration officials felt that guaranteed employment or a guaranteed income was highly desirable, the Johnson Administration made no attempt to formulate such policy for political consideration. A crude but useful demographic analysis of the Ninetieth Congress suggests what limits policy formulators must face when they address themselves to an area perceived as an *urban* problem. Most Congressmen come from areas where this urban problem does not

[1] See Peter Bachrach and Morton S. Baratz, "Decisions and non-Decisions: An Analytical Framework," *American Political Science Review*, LVII (September, 1963), 641–642.

72

exist. Thus, in the Ninetieth Congress, only 115, or 26.5 percent, of the 435 Congressmen had a majority of constituents who, by the 1960 Census, lived in central cities of over 50,000. Another 97, or 22.2 percent, had a majority of constituents who lived in urbanized areas (central cities of over 50,000 *and* their surrounding suburbs) but not a majority living in the central cities alone. Seventy-five of these latter districts were more suburban than urban in character. Although it is true that not all suburbs perceive their interests to be antithetical to central cities, it seems beyond question that large numbers of these suburban districts shared neither the problems nor the concern of the central cities. A clear majority of the Congressional districts—223, or 51.7 percent—were primarily small town or rural.[2]

However, Congress, or elements of it, can, at times, act as a prod on the Administration to formulate more aggressive housing policy. Thus, liberal Congressmen may grab the initiative and attempt to develop policy themselves, as Senators Walter Mondale (D–Minn.) and Charles Percy (R–Ill.) did in 1967 with their homeownership for low-income people proposals. These proposals generated wide, favorable publicity and literally forced the Administration[3] to include a home-ownership program in the 1968 bill.

Institutional factors also affect the formulation of policy. Entrenched segments within the HUD bureaucracy may resist new or changing programs which disrupt existing patterns of relationships. The Public Housing Administration vigorously, though unsuccessfully, fought the rent-supplement program because it perceived this program as a threat to its own existence. Similarly, questions of institutional self-interest may move other agencies to oppose certain types of policy. Thus, the Treasury Department actively dis-

[2] These figures were compiled by Henry Bain and Mrs. Carol Kimbrough of the Washington Center for Metropolitan Studies.

[3] Secretary Weaver had originally vigorously opposed homeownership for the poor on the grounds that it would impair labor mobility and that, at any rate, poor people should not be saddled with such large debts. See U.S. Congress, Senate Subcommittee on Housing and Urban Affairs, Committee on Banking and Currency, *Hearings on Housing Legislation of 1967*, 90th Cong., 1st Sess. (1967), Part 1, p. 8.

courages attempts to use the tax structure for social purposes such as helping house the poor. In 1967, for example, Under Secretary of the Treasury Joseph Barr testified in opposition to Senator Robert Kennedy's bill which utilized tax credits to encourage investment in low-income housing. Barr and Senator Smathers (D–Fla.), a co-sponsor of the Kennedy proposal, tangled.

MR. BARR: . . . We have consistently opposed the use of the tax code for narrow or specialized purposes. In this situation, we are considering a problem that involves urban housing, but not all urban housing. We are considering a problem that involves a portion of urban housing.

SENATOR SMATHERS: . . . Is it your judgment and the Treasury's judgment that the riots in Newark and Detroit are a specialized problem that is not of concern to the Treasury and the people of the United States?

MR. BARR: . . . It is indeed of concern to the Treasury and to every reasonable man in this country. It must be attacked. The only issue we are raising here: Is the tax code the appropriate vehicle? [4]

The Labor Department attempts to stymie proposals that are anathema to organized labor and ensures that prevailing union wage rates be paid for any construction financed with federal monies. OEO, for its part, attempts to ensure that housing programs involve adequate participation of the poor.

Many lobby groups, particularly the ones that have an important political impact (U.S. Conference of Mayors, National League of Cities, and organized labor) also put a rather constant pressure on the institutionalized presidency. The form of this pressure from the above three groups has almost always been in terms of making more money available to cities with as few strings attached as possible. Since this input is, in effect, a constant factor, it is largely ineffective unless combined with other forces.

Of the housing industry groups, the National Association of Home Builders appeared, at least during the mid-1960's, to have exercised the greatest impact on the formulation of policy. The Home Builders, because of the fragmented nature of the industry,

[4] U.S. Congress, Senate Committee on Finance, *Hearings on S. 2100, Tax Incentives to Encourage Housing in Urban Poverty Areas*, 90th Cong., 1st Sess. (1967), p. 148.

represent political power in nearly every Congressional district. For this reason, the Administration was quite willing to listen to (and even incorporate) the ideas of NAHB in exchange for the Home Builders' support in Congress, particularly since in broad terms, NAHB goals (more home ownership) coincided generally with the Administration's goals. NAHB, at least during the mid-1960's, further pyramided their influence by electing prominent Democrats to head their organization, including Larry Blackmon, a Texan and close personal friend of President Johnson.

More narrowly oriented groups with housing concerns (Mortgage Bankers Association, American Bankers Association, United States Savings and Loan Associations, etc.) had little impact on Administration policy formulation, at least so far as major redistributive policy is concerned. Rather these groups work either through the Congressional committees or the HUD bureaucracy in an effort to achieve their more limited ends. A few organizations which would like to influence redistributive policy, such as the National Association of Housing and Redevelopment Officials (NAHRO), complain bitterly that the process of Administration policy formulation does not provide them the access they feel they deserve.

A variety of semiorganized elites also operate in the policy-formulation environment. Some businessmen, for instance, responded to the President's plea for a "constructive" partnership with government in housing ventures. These businessmen pressed the President to devise programs attractive to private industry, and the President, in turn, pressed them to become more active in social concerns. The Business Advisory Council provided the formal link between the Administration and business, but informal contacts between the President and businessmen such as Edgar Kaiser of Kaiser Industries, Ben Heineman of the Chicago and Northwestern Railroad, and David Rockefeller of the Chase Manhattan Bank were probably more important.

In a more diffuse sense, academics (such as Charles Abrams and Anthony Downs, semipopular urbanologists (such as Daniel Moynihan), and popularizers (such as Jane Jacobs) occupied an important place in the environment, because their writings in some ways provided the common experience for those within the system, and thus shaped the framework of policy. In addition, these writings provided a source of new ideas and proposals in the field of housing.

## Conversion Process: Congressional Initiative

Since 1964 the institutionalized presidency has been the major source of policy initiation in housing. Prior to that, Congress and HHFA's general counsel's office and office of program policy played the major role. In most cases, however, decisions emanating from those bodies were not redistributive in nature, although there are significant exceptions. One such exception was the Housing Act of 1949, which laid the basis for urban renewal. This was largely a product of years of work by the Senate Banking and Currency Committee, particularly by Senators Taft (R–Ohio) and Wagner (D–N.Y.). In 1954 President Eisenhower anticipated the *modus operandi* of later Democratic presidents, by presenting to Congress a program (involving some redistributive change) based on recommendations of the Advisory Committee on Government Housing Policies and Programs, appointed in 1953. After 1954, however, Eisenhower began to favor less involvement of the federal government in housing. As a result, the initiative in housing legislation switched back to Congress, particularly to the Housing Subcommittee of the House Banking and Currency Committee, which was chaired by Albert Rains (D–Ala.) and staffed by John Barriere. The combination of a reluctant Republican President and a strong Democratic leadership in a Democratic Congress, greatly enhanced the power of Congress; but, again, mostly for distributive changes. The distributive nature of the changes is underlined by the frequent use of omnibus housing bills, which serve to facilitate the something-for-everybody "disaggregated" trading and bargaining characteristic of distributive change.

After 1964 this pattern changed for a variety of reasons which will be discussed later. However, the shift coincided with the retirement of Representative Rains and the reorganization of HHFA into HUD. The latter resulted in the departure of the powerful General Counsel, Milton Semer, and a clear downgrading of that division within the housing agency.

Despite the relative decline in the importance of Congress as the initiator of policy, it may still effectively involve itself in policy formulation under certain conditions.

When the Administration itself puts forth no proposal, there is a policy vacuum waiting to be filled. Senator Charles Percy filled that vacuum in 1967. Percy, a Republican freshman from Illinois, announced plans for a major housing bill almost as soon as he entered the Senate, and because he was at that time regarded as a possible Republican Presidential candidate for 1968, his proposal received wide publicity. The Percy bill would have established a private nonprofit foundation, which would have been capitalized through federally guaranteed bonds. The foundation would have been able to provide nonprofit sponsors with low-interest loans for rehabilitating or constructing homes for resale to low-income families. The eventual low-income homeowner would have received his mortgage at below-market interest rates with a direct subsidy from the Treasury making up the difference.

The bill was one especially appealing to Republicans searching for alternatives to Democratic proposals, since it emphasized homeownership (one of the traditional American virtues according to Republican ideology), and since it worked as closely as possible through the private market. The bill was introduced April 20, 1967, in both the Senate and the House. All thirty-six of the Republican senators co-sponsored the bill, while 106 of the 187 Republicans in the House did likewise. Senator Dirksen (R–Ill.) the Republican minority leader, termed the bill "the major Republican housing measure in this session." [5]

Meanwhile, three Democratic senators (Clark, Mondale, and Ri-

---

[5] "Republican Housing Bill Introduced in Both Chambers," *Congressional Quarterly*, April 28, 1967, p. 687.

bicoff) had introduced separate bills, each providing for low-income homeownership. Although the three bills varied, they all differed from the Percy proposal in one major aspect: all worked through the existing FHA structure rather than through a new private foundation. Mondale's bill was the result of close cooperation between the Senator's staff and John Zuccoti, an assistant to HUD Undersecretary Robert Wood. Wood, according to a respondent, wished to assure a Democratic alternative to the Percy bill. The Administration, for its part, did not submit any major proposals in the housing field during 1967. As a result, Chairman John Sparkman (D–Ala.) was free to hold hearings on the homeownership proposals. Sparkman, according to several respondents, decided to hold the hearings partly because of the publicity engendered by Percy's proposals and partly because the numerous homeownership proposals by Democrats indicated a real Senate interest in that concept.

The hearings started July 17, and the Administration opposition was quickly indicated by Secretary Weaver, who contended the Percy measure would not serve low-income people, since total monthly payments would still be over $100 a month for a $12,500 home. Weaver also questioned whether low-income people ought to be saddled with the debt homeownership would occasion, and whether their marginal employment situation put a premium on mobility which homeownership would greatly hinder.[6] Those close to Weaver were unanimous in agreeing that Weaver's opposition to homeownership by the poor was real in substantive terms and that it was not occasioned solely by the fact that the proposal had been identified with a possible Republican Presidential contender. However, according to a HUD official, opposition from the White House did seem predicated on political considerations.

After the hearings, Senator Sparkman directed Carl Coan, the staff director of the Senate Housing Subcommittee, to prepare a

[6] *Hearings on House Legislation of 1967, op. cit.* (n. 3).

draft bill based on the best in all four proposals. Coan, working closely with Ashley Foard of HUD's General Counsel's office, settled on a proposal which embodied the main feature of Senator Mondale's bill—direct federal subsidy of interest payments on FHA mortgages to low-income homeowners. At that point, Sparkman urged Percy and Mondale to agree on a compromise proposal using the committee's bill as a starting point.

Coan; John MacGuire, Mondale's legislative assistant; and Carol Khosrovi, Percy's assistant, then met several times to try to work out an agreement. Late in the year, Senators Sparkman, Mondale, and Percy met with Secretary Weaver; Philip Brownstein, the Assistant Secretary for FHA; Joseph Barr, Undersecretary of the Treasury; Sherman Maisel of the Federal Reserve Board; and Charles Schultze, Director of the Budget Bureau. At that meeting Weaver endorsed, for the first time, a small homeownership program. Sparkman also suggested what would eventually be the means to a compromise solution. Percy had held out for funding through his private foundation because FHA money, strangled by a 6 percent maximum interest rate, was becoming scarce, as interest rates soared in the economy. Sparkman suggested the interest rate on FHA loans be temporarily freed to make FHA money available, and Percy agreed. The eventual compromise—worked out between Mondale, Percy, MacGuire, and Khosrovi—satisfied Percy by keeping in the bill his National Homeownership Foundation, although that foundation was now limited to providing technical advice to private and public organizations to help promote homeownership among low-income people. The financing mechanism was basically drawn from the original Mondale proposal.

On November 28, 1967, the Banking and Currency Committee reported out S.2700, the Percy-Mondale compromise on homeownership. However, political factors in the House prevented Sparkman from bringing the bill to the floor in that session. The 1968 Administration bill (according to several respondents, the President himself was committed to the idea of homeownership for the poor), for all practical purposes, incorporated S.2700 as its home-ownership proposal.[7]

Congress also may have a major impact on policy formulation in somewhat different circumstances. Thus, working within the framework of an omnibus housing bill, Congressmen may pledge their support for an Administration bill in return for inclusion in that bill of their own pet proposals.

William Widnall (R–N.J.) ranking Republican member of the House Banking and Currency Subcommittee on Housing, was the foremost exponent of this form of Congressional policy formulation. In 1964, Widnall inserted a proposal for 3 percent rehabilitation loans for slum homeowners, and in 1965 he was responsible for the rent-certificate program, through which existing units of housing are rented by the government from private landlords for public housing. Both were successfully enacted, and both are major programs, at least semiredistributive in nature.

In order for Congress to exercise an impact in this manner, however, two conditions must be met. First, the Administration and Congressional leadership must be convinced that the support of

[7] It is probably fair to say that Senator Percy, despite the fact that very little of his original proposal remained in the bill, was the man most responsible for the 1968 homeownership legislation. Certainly he was the necessary, if clearly not sufficient, cause. Yet, it is interesting to reflect on what chance conditions a major piece of housing legislation rested. The 1968 homeownership legislation rested ultimately on the fact that Charles Percy's family was, during his Depression childhood, evicted from several apartments for nonpayment of rent. This, according to Percy at a speech before the National Housing Conference's Convention in April 1967, accounted for his interest in housing and homeownership in particular, rather than in some other area of legislation.

The influence of individual personalities is a recurring theme throughout an analysis of the housing policy process. Undoubtedly, broader forces determine what is possible and what is not; but the force of individual personality—the right man in the right place at the right time—is in good part responsible for whether what is possible does indeed occur, and for, with a good deal of latitude, what shape it actually takes when it does occur. That this is, in many ways, alien to the analytical framework of social scientists, ought not to obscure the fact that it is so. Although ultimately explainable and classifiable perhaps by reference to psychological variables, it may be useful to view personality, at least given the present state of social science knowledge, as essentially a random variable.

someone like Widnall is necessary in order to assure passage of the Administration's proposals. Second, there must be in that key position a Congressman with personal and staff resources sufficient to present a cogent housing proposal and, given the complexity of housing policy, this condition will not always be satisfied.

The more normal manner of Congressional policy formulation involves distributive policy included at the behest of housing groups which maintain close liaison with members of the committees and committee staff. These groups provide needed technical information to Congressional personnel and, in return, hope to be granted favorable consideration on rather technical policy of great importance to them, but of relatively little importance to other powerful groups.

## Conversion Process: The Institutionalized Presidency Initiative

Despite the important role Congress can play in policy formulation, the more normal vehicle, at least since 1964, has been the institutionalized Presidency—White House staff, Bureau of the Budget, Council of Economic Advisors, and special White House task forces—with particular emphasis on the task force. Although the processes of policy formulation have varied widely since 1964, the skeletal form utilized by the Johnson Administration is readily visible. The process, moreover, appeared similar for all areas of domestic policy, including housing. In late spring, Presidential Special Assistant Joseph Califano and his assistants would travel to a number of universities in order to glean ideas for new programs. They talked to people in a variety of disciplines, asking them to discuss a specific problem (such as cities or housing) or to discuss what they felt the country's pressing problems were. After returning, Califano would write a letter to each of the people who had been met with, asking each to submit proposals for solutions to the problems that had been discussed. These were compiled in a single book which formed the basis for discussion by top representatives of the institutionalized Presidency concerning priorities for developing legislation for the following year. In July and August, Califano, in a series of meetings, discussed the compiled proposals with the President. In some cases, new, outside task forces would be set up; in other cases, proposals would be sent to relevant agencies, and occasionally some of the proposals would be completely abandoned. The task forces met and generally submitted their reports to the White House by November. The White House then sent the reports to the Budget Bureau for evaluation and to other relevant agencies for comment.

The next step was to develop the reports' recommendations into legislative proposals, if legislation was desired (there were significant Administration housing proposals in 1965, 1966, and 1968). This process was accomplished in December, during a series of meetings coordinated by the White House. Participants were top officials (or their representatives) of the institutionalized Presidency.[8] In housing policy, those present usually included William Moyers or Califano; a White House assistant for urban affairs (Richard Goodwin; or, later, Fred Bohen); the Director of the Budget Bureau (first, Kermit Gordon; then, Charles Schultze) and his top expert in housing (Philip Hanna); the top urban expert on the Council of Economic Advisers (James S. Duesenberry); plus Secretary Weaver and Undersecretary Wood (another functional member of the institutionalized Presidency, appointed by Johnson from an academic post at M.I.T.). High-ranking officials of other departments, such as Undersecretary of the Treasury Joseph Barr, might also be present when matters of concern to their institutions were under discussion.

After agreement was reached, the White House representative

---

[8] In such cases, it seems useful to include Secretary Weaver as a member of the institutionalized Presidency, since not only was he a direct Presidential appointment, but due to his lack of strong support from clientele groups, he was dependent on the President a great deal more than most Cabinet secretaries. In short, Weaver's strength was that he was the Negro in Johnson's cabinet; his weakness was that Negro groups did not solidly support him on substantive issues.

(Moyers or Califano) presented the proposals to the President for his approval or reshaping. The President made the final decision late in December or early in January in time for inclusion in his State of the Union address. The latter was a joint product of the White House, Budget Bureau, and HUD.

## Conversion Process: The Task Force

The task force operation was the crux of the entire process. Task forces were not, of course, unknown before President Johnson, but they were never used as widely nor as explicitly as a formal means of policy formulation before his administration. The immediate inspiration for the task force concept seems to have been the Kennedy preinaugural experience in 1961. At that time the President-elect set up academic task forces in a number of areas, one of which was housing. As one member of the 1961 task force put it, "It was an attempt to mobilize a series of propositions that the bureaucracy would have to respond to."

However, the 1961 housing task force was not a very important factor in formulating the 1961 housing proposals. Instead, the 1961 proposals were put together by the newly appointed HHFA staff and Budget Bureau representatives in a series of meetings chaired by Robert Weaver. The principal proposal was the 221 (d) (3) moderate-income rental program, which was largely the result of the thinking of General Counsel Milton Semer, FHA Commissioner Neil Hardy, and Assistant Administrator Morton J. Schussheim. The White House simply accepted Agency recommendations because, as a participant recalled, "They had no urbanist or housing man on their staff. We dealt with Lee White, who knew something about housing, but who certainly was no expert."

The 1961 housing task force's lack of influence is traceable to the fact that it was composed mostly of outsiders who had no institutional attachments to the policy process. The chairman of the task force was Joseph McMurray, who had been commissioner of housing in New York. As one respondent remarked, "Had McMurray been appointed head of HHFA, as he hoped to be, or had Weaver been chairman of that task force before being appointed Administrator, then that task force report would have counted for something, because there would have been someone with power pushing it. As it was, it could be safely ignored."

√ No major housing proposals emerged from 1962–64, although in 1964 a series of rather incremental proposals emerged largely from HHFA's office of program policy. The next important legislation, that of 1965, came out of the first round of Johnson task forces, established in 1964. That housing task force, chaired by Robert Wood, was extragovernmental, composed mostly of academics and experts, as the 1961 Kennedy task forces had been. As several respondents suggested, President Johnson felt he had to go outside the Administration if he were to develop his own proposals, since many of his top officials had been inherited from the Kennedy Administration. The 1964 task force recommended the rent-supplement proposal, which Congress enacted into law in 1965.

In 1965, the task force was, according to one respondent, "a refinement of the 1964 one, more consistent with the Johnson style. The '65 group was, again, mostly extra-governmental but unlike the '64 one, its membership reflected major centers of power in American society. The President himself took a much greater interest in the '65 task force, which recommended both the Model Cities program (enacted into law in 1966) and the organization of the new Department of Housing and Urban development." (See p. 91 for a list of the membership of the 1965 task force.)

The 1966 task force, the Ylvisaker task force, followed on the heels of two very productive predecessors in terms of legislative achievements. Since the political climate did not appear propitious for further legislation, the 1966 task force—which, like the 1964 task force, was topheavy with academics—was not aimed specifically at developing legislation for 1967. Instead, it produced a document that, as one observer commented, was more philosophic than legislative. The Ylvisaker report concentrated on the problems of racism in American society rather than on urbanism, which had preoccupied HUD and its predecessors during the preceding years. There is widespread agreement that the report had little, if any, policy impact because, as several respondents indicated, its recommendations were simply "too radical."

Three task forces were in operation in 1967: the Douglas Commission, the Kaiser Committee, and an intragovernment interagency task force. Both the Kaiser and Douglas commissions were public bodies composed of representatives of various segments of American society. The Douglas Commission was created by Congress in 1966 mainly to study problems of new development such as zoning, building codes, taxation, and other related problems. It quickly expanded its purview to include inner-city problems and conducted a series of public hearings in cities around the country. Since it had no real institutional Presidency base, and since its chairman, former Senator Paul Douglas, alienated HUD officials with his public criticism of the Department, the commission contributed little to policy.

The Kaiser Committee (The President's Committee on Urban Housing—see p. 91 for a list of the membership) was established with much fanfare by the President, and was charged specifically with developing proposals to increase the production of housing for low-and moderate-income families. Its major substantive contribution was Title IX of the Administration's 1968 housing legislation, a proposal for a National Housing Partnership (which was a private corporation to provide equity capital for low- and moderate-income housing). The Kaiser Committee also set the national housing goal of twenty-six million houses over the next decade, which the President announced in his State of the Union message. HUD had submitted a substantially smaller figure.

The 1967 interagency governmental task force probably had the greatest input on the Administration's 1968 proposals, apart from the National Housing Partnership proposal and the homeownership proposal, which emanated from the Senate Housing Subcommittee.[9] Members of the task force chaired and dominated by HUD included representatives of seven departments or agencies, plus

---

[9] According to a member of the institutionalized Presidency, it was these two proposals which the President thought most important.

representatives of the institutionalized Presidency. It was this task force which advocated, for the first time, the setting of national housing goals. It also recommended a new homeownership program which was strikingly similar to the one drawn up in the Senate Housing Subcommittee and a new rent-supplement approach through interest subsidies on mortgages. The President, particularly because he chose to make housing his major domestic legislation in 1968, kept in close touch with the task force through the participation of Joseph Califano's assistant, Fred Bohen.

## Task Force Functions

Members of the institutionalized Presidency viewed the task force as a major institutional innovation of the Johnson Administration. A high official in the Executive Offices commented:

Starting in 1964, the White House took a much greater role than it had in the past in the formulation of new legislation. Previously, the Budget Bureau had formally called on the Department for submission of new legislation. This tended to bring forth either pet unworkable ideas or minor variations—but not really significant changes. The task force process put the White House, to some extent the Budget Bureau, and to a lesser extent, the Council of Economic Advisers in the driver's seat. Within that framework, some departments have responded better than others in terms of producing change. HEW is a good example, although real big changes don't come from them. HUD perhaps is a little worse than others.

Despite this view, it appears that task forces were, even in the Johnson Administration, in many ways a response to felt needs rather than an institutionalized form of policy formulation. The task force concept provides a useful means of developing policy proposals when new proposals are needed and when, for whatever reasons, such proposals cannot be trusted or expected to come from within the Administration itself. This is likely to occur in three situations, two of which were clearly present when Johnson initiated the task force operation in 1964. In the first case, a Vice President succeeding to the Presidency during the term of his predecessor [10] obviously finds himself in a situation in which the Administration, at least at first, is not his own. In such cases, the new President may go outside to develop his own policy proposals rather than have them associated with his predecessor. Several respondents suggested that this factor accounted in large measure for the 1964 Johnson task forces. As one observed, "He inherited a lot of Kennedy blood and he didn't trust it."

In the second case, a department or agency may develop its own interests independent of those of the President. This may occur particularly after top officials have held their position for several years and have developed a loyalty to their agency rather than to the Presidency. Questions of institutional self-preservation may conflict with Presidential desires for policy change. In 1964, for instance, top HHFA personnel had remained stable for nearly four years. A rather uneasy equilibrium relationship had been established between HHFA and the various power centers (Congressional substantive and Appropriations Committees, various financially oriented clientele groups, etc.) involved in distributive housing policy. The White House wished to disturb this equilibrium by initiating new redistributive policies. According to several respondents, HHFA opposed the 1964 rent-supplement proposals on the grounds that Congress would never buy them as a substitute for the popular 221 (d) (3) program. HHFA then opposed the 1965 model cities proposals because it felt its position was not strong enough to withstand another major Congressional battle after the rent-supplement struggle the previous year. In both cases, top HHFA personnel also were uneasy about the substantive desirability of the legislation.

Conversely, at the beginning of an Administration when loyalty to the President on the part of recent personal appointees is likely

[10] Such an occurrence ought to be viewed by political scientists as a normal occurrence in American politics rather than as an aberration. In this century, four of our twelve Presidents (Theodore Roosevelt, Coolidge, Truman, and Johnson) have succeeded to that office from the Vice-Presidency after the death of a President. In two other cases (Wilson and Eisenhower), the Vice-President certainly came close to succeeding to the Presidency.

to be high, and ideas fresh, task forces may not be as important as the department or agency. In 1961, the newly appointed HHFA leadership ignored the report of a special housing task force and submitted his own proposals which the President then embraced as Administration policy.

The third case for task forces as a means of developing policy proposals is the official rationale given publicly by the Administration: task forces are called upon when a problem exists and there is no obvious answer to it. This has not frequently been the case in housing, where a common cliché is that there is no such thing as a new idea. However, it appears more frequently in other areas. As an Executive Office respondent recalled, the 1966 task force on children came forth with suggestions that could not have been developed inside the government, simply because the best minds in the country were put to work on the problem in the task force. Thus, task forces can provide the President with views of problems and ideas for solving them that perhaps are unavailable elsewhere —either because expertise is not available or because political considerations prevent bringing the idea to the President's attention. In language very close to that which Richard Neustadt uses in *Presidential Power* (1964), a member of the institutionalized Presidency commented, "The President has simply got to have advice from someone who really knows what the right answer is and who has no political axe to grind."

By the same token, when answers were known, the White House was likely to utilize inside interagency task forces to develop proposals. Thus, the President, in 1967, determined that housing programs must be greatly speeded up, and directed an interagency task force to develop the bulk of the Administration's proposals for 1968. That it was called an interagency task force, however, should not disguise the fact that it was very much dominated by HUD.

## Varieties of Task Forces

Since 1964, three distinctive types of task forces could be discerned in the area of housing policy. Most publicized has been the public commission, composed of distinguished representatives of various sectors of American society plus, in certain cases, a sprinkling of academics or experts (in order, as one respondent suggested, to make sure there are some ideas). The Kaiser Committee and the Douglas Commission in housing are good examples of this type of commission, as are the Kerner Commission on civil disorders, the Heineman Commission on income maintenance, and the Crime Commission. A second type is the nonpublic task force composed either of representatives of sectors in American society (the 1965 Wood task force) or mainly of academics (1964 Wood task force, Ylvisaker task force). Finally, there is the interagency task force (1967 HUD task force).

The public commissions can, as cynics have suggested, give the illusion that something is being done to attack a problem. Creating a public commission or task force is a safe response; it gives the appearance of action and yet at the same time it disturbs none of the very real political opposition which would emerge if substantive action were attempted.[11] The impact of the report of such a commission is likely to be more in terms of public education than immediate Administration policy proposals, unless the President is utterly certain of the task force chairman and keeps in close contact with him. The Kaiser Committee was a good example of such an exception. Both Kaiser and staff director Howard Moscof remained in close contact with the White House and, as has already been pointed out, had an immediate impact upon Administration policy.

[11] Elizabeth Drew lists, in a barbed though highly perceptive article, eight uses of public commissions. Among these are: to postpone action, yet be justified in insisting that you are at work on the problem; to act as a lightning rod, drawing political heat away from the White House; to investigate, lay to rest rumors, and convince the public of the validity of one particular set of facts. See Elizabeth Drew, "On Giving Oneself a Hotfoot: Government by Commission," *Atlantic Monthly*, CCXXI, No. 5 (May, 1968), 45–48.

A highly placed official in the Executive Office of the President remarked, "There's a hell of a lot of truth to some of the things in Drew's article. However, in some cases we do expect new and important things to come out of public commissions. In some cases we do it publicly because we want to expose the report to a lot of public attention. In the process of making recommendations, we then build support."

The less public task forces are likely to be much more effective, however. As a member of the institutionalized Presidency observed, "The more inside the task force, the more serious its results are likely to be. The process of policy formulation is one no public servant likes to see done in the open. It's a little bit like the professional diplomat's aversion to open diplomacy." Of particular importance are the nonpublic, outside task forces, which share with the commissions the attribute of representativeness.

The benefits derived from a "representative" outside task force are several. Most important, if the task force report is unanimous, a supporting coalition representing most of the major elements in American society will already have been built. Issues dividing builders, labor, financiers, cities, civil rights groups, and others will have been bargained out and settled prior to the Congressional battle, where the Administration has much less control. In 1965, for example, rent-supplements legislation came out of a nonrepresentative academic task force in 1964, and was significantly changed by Congress. The 1966 model cities legislation, on the other hand, coming from the 1965 Wood "representative" task force, emerged from Congress relatively similar to the legislation which the Administration had submitted. In addition, business support for model cities was led by Ben Heineman, a member of the 1965 task force.

Representative task forces (and representative public commissions) have the added benefit of co-opting relatively powerful but essentially conservative elements of society into directing their efforts toward social problem-solving. That this is a conscious and explicit function of these task forces was suggested by a high official in the institutionalized Presidency, who volunteered: "We try to bring some of these elements in to, in effect, co-opt them. We rub their noses in the problem and bring them along with the solutions. Hell, some of them have never seen slums or ghettos before. We bring them in to the slums and they are amazed that such things can exist. It's surprising how radical some of them become."

The membership of the two "representative" task forces and

commissions gives a good indication of what segments of American society are and are not included.

## Wood Task Force (1965)

ROBERT WOOD, Political Science Department, M.I.T. (academic)

CHARLES HAAR, Harvard Law School (academic)

KERMIT GORDON, Director, Bureau of the Budget (President)

BEN HEINEMAN, President, Chicago and Northwestern Railroad (business)

EDGAR KAISER, President, Kaiser Industries (business)

WALTER REUTHER, President, United Auto Workers (labor)

WILLIAM RAFSKY, Executive Vice President, Old Philadelphia Development Corporation (cities)

WHITNEY YOUNG, Executive Director, Urban League (Negroes)

SENATOR ABRAHAM RIBICOFF (D–Conn.), United States Senate (Congress)

## Kaiser Committee (1967–68)

EDGAR KAISER, President, Kaiser Industries (business)

GRAHAM MORGAN, President, U.S. Gypsum (business)

J. IRWIN MILLER, President, Cummins Engine Co. (business)

LEON WEINER, Past President, National Association of Homebuilders (small builder)

CHARLES KELLER, Association of General Contractors (small builder)

RAYMOND NASHER, President, Nasher Industries (small builder)

R. V. HANSBERGER, President, Boise Cascade Corporation (large builder)

PETER KIEWIT, President, Peter Kiewit Sons (large builder)

S. B. BECHTEL, President, Bechtel Corporation (large builder)

GAYLORD FREEMAN, Vice-Chairman, First National Bank of Washington (finance)

JOHN MC CONE, Joshua Hend Corporation (finance)

JOHN WHEELER, President, Mechanics and Farmers Bank, Durham, N.C. (finance and a Negro)

GEORGE MEANY, President, AFL-CIO (craft and guild unions)

JOSEPH KEENAN, Secretary, International Brotherhood of Electrical Workers (craft and guild unions)

WALTER REUTHER, President, United Auto Workers (industrial unions)

WHITNEY YOUNG, Executive Director, National Urban League (Negro organization)

JOSEPH BARR, Mayor of Pittsburgh (cities)

WALTER ROSENBLITH, Professor of Communications Biophysics, M.I.T. (academic)

In a loose way the members do represent their institutional bases during task force or commission deliberations. Indeed, a staff member of one of the task forces commented, "They not only actually do speak in terms of the interests of that sector of society from which they are appointed, but in many cases they perceive their role on the task force as doing exactly that." In the 1965 Wood task force, according to a participant in the proceedings, Kermit Gordon, the Director of the Budget, spoke frequently in terms of budgetary considerations and restraints; Senator Ribicoff (and his assistant, Jerome Sonofsky) viewed things in terms of political constraints imposed by Congress. It was Ribicoff who suggested that the number of model cities demonstration projects be increased from the initial six or even to seventy in order to scatter them in more states and thus increase the legislation's Congressional market ability. William Rafsky looked after the interests of cities vis-à-vis metropolitan areas and Charles Haar spoke often in terms of legal considerations. Walter Reuther promoted a system approach which would create an industrialized prefab housing industry. Robert Wood, the chairman, talked in terms of general policy considerations and directed the discussion, but it was Ben Heineman who played the essential role of broker. "He was the guy who managed to find the formula to please all, who came up with the compromise that made sense."

In the Kaiser Committee deliberations, a major dispute broke down along the lines of small builders (Leon Weiner, Charles

Keller, and Raymond Nasher) vs. large builders (Edgar Kaiser, Peter Kiewit) who wanted to create a huge and monolithic housing industry.[12] The industrial unions (Walter Reuther) sympathized with the idea of creating a real housing industry, while the crafts and guilds (George Meany and Joseph Keenan) opposed. According to an observer, "The bankers generally acted like bankers and the Negroes talk about equal access and citizen participation."

Generally, the representative task forces and commissions seemed to confirm a trend which Theodore Lowi has called "Interest Group Liberalism." As an example of this, Lowi quotes Arthur Schlesinger, Jr., describing the Administration of John Kennedy: "What is the essence of a multi-interest Administration? It is surely that the leading interests in society are all represented in the interior process of policy formation which can be done only if members or advocates of these interests are included in key positions of government." [13]

Some outside task forces, such as the 1964 Wood task force and the 1966 Ylvisaker task force, were primarily academic in nature. Academic task forces were more likely to be used by Johnson when no immediate legislation was envisioned, but when a longer-range view was required.[14] Academic task forces are suspect by members of the institutionalized Presidency because of the faults usually attributed to academics. They are "not practical" according to one; they have no sense of political reality according to another. Thus, the Ylvisaker report was criticized by a member of HUD as "completely useless. It was simply too radical." Since 1964, according to a member of the White House circle, conscious attempts have been made to ensure that "a few practical men [translate "nonacademics"] are on those task forces which are predominantly academic."

---

[12] The small builders won.

[13] Theodore Lowi, "The Public Philosophy: Interest Group Liberalism," *American Political Science Review*, LXI, (March, 1967), 5–24.

[14] The 1964 Wood task force is an exception since it had immediate legislative impact. However, the experience with the full range of task forces in 1964 led to a deemphasis on primarily academic task forces, according to a member of the Executive Office of the President.

Interagency task forces, as has already been suggested, were, at least in the Johnson Administration, a main mechanism of policy formulation only when the President either already knew what he wanted in the form of legislation or, alternatively, did not want much of anything. In 1967, according to a high official in the Executive Office of the President, the President determined to put major effort into housing for the 1968 legislative program, mostly in terms of gearing up and improving present programs to a level where they could produce far more than they had in the past. He asked Presidential Special Assistant Joseph Califano to set up an interagency task force through HUD to put together proposals.

The *raison d'etre* of the interagency task force is the belief that functional problems cut across departmental lines. Thus, housing problems are at the same time problems for OEO and HEW as well as HUD. This belief, however, although perhaps publicly shared by the departments, privately often runs counter to each department's view of its own interests. Thus, a former HUD employee described some interagency task force meetings he attended as "fluff, speeches, an exchange of papers, but most of all lies. The various agencies strive to protect their own jurisdictions. They are imperialistic and it is difficult to get any kind of results from them. They will work only if Califano rides them and makes it known he wants results."

In 1967, Califano did let it be known that he wanted results from the interagency housing task force. In all, six departments or agencies, plus representatives of the institutionalized Presidency, had representation on the task force,[15] but the results were not a testimony to the interagency nature of the group. The membership and the staff were left to the discretion of HUD's Secretary Robert Weaver, who chaired the task force himself and staffed it with two of his special assistants, Jay Janis and Henry Schechter. According to all accounts, HUD—and Weaver in particular—dominated the proceedings and wrote most of the papers, including the final re-

[15] HUD, Commerce, Treasury, Justice, OEO, HEW, Budget Bureau, Council of Economic Advisers, and the White House staff.

port. As an observer remarked: "Interagency task forces often simply reflect the lead agency's legislative program. Last fall HUD did all the staff work and Weaver chaired. The result would have been about the same had it simply come out of HUD without the participation of other agencies."

## Task Force Operations and Procedures

The membership of the task forces was selected by means of rather informal nominations from members of the White House staff, Budget Bureau, Council of Economic Advisers, and during the last part of the Johnson Administration, the Secretary and Undersecretary of HUD. A participant in one of these sessions described the criteria used for nominations: "The names were suggested on the basis of a kind of common-sense soundness. We would not have picked a Michael Harrington, for example. We looked for people who had written with perspective but reasonable freshness and who hadn't been in the Government for several years."

About fifty names were gathered from these sources and they were then winnowed down, with the White House representative playing the dominant role. At that point, Califano would send the list to the President, who generally approved most of the members and, in some cases, made his own additions. In 1965, for example, it was President Johnson himself who was responsible for the inclusion of Senator Ribicoff and Edgar Kaiser on the Wood task force. The overlap in actual membership between task forces (for example, four members of the 1965 Wood task force were later members of the Kaiser Committee) reinforces the tongue-in-cheek conclusion of Elizabeth Drew that "a study of rosters of recently appointed commissions tends to confirm the widely held view that there are only forty-seven people in the whole world." [16]

All the task forces, including the public commissions, were shrouded in a good deal of secrecy while preparing their reports.

[16] Drew, *op. cit.* (n. 11), p. 48.

The reports and even the membership of the nonpublic task forces have never been publicly released and are treated in the same manner as classified national security material. A staff member on one of the task forces commented, "Our task force was a CIA-like operation. I felt very odd about it. I wasn't sure what I could say and what I couldn't." The secrecy was justified by the Administration as a means of assuring a creative flow of ideas to the President without necessarily committing him to them or embarrassing him politically. According to all who have participated on task forces, members were given nearly complete freedom to come forth with ideas. The President, observed a high official in the Executive Offices, wanted their judgment on substance—not priority or political feasibility. The task force members were thus told to ignore the latter two considerations and concentrate on the former. In 1965, for example, the task force was told to come up with, in the words of one participant, "a bold new experimental program which would dramatically revitalize large areas of the city. The only decisions that had been made were that it would be a demonstration program and it would involve competition among cities for grants." As one Budget Bureau official observed: "The task forces have a lot of freedom to come up with new ideas. Probably they have too much freedom. In many cases, the report just gets buried. But they can come up with whatever they want. That's the beauty of confidential reports."

The actual proceedings of the task forces reflected both similarities and differences associated with the various types of task forces. All apparently operated on the basis of prepared papers (by the staff in the more prestigious commissions and task forces; by the members themselves in some of the more academic-oriented and interagency task forces), discussion based on the papers, and then revision. In all cases, decisions were arrived at by consensus, often after prolonged discussion and compromise. The consensual process was aided by what appears to be the informal decision rule that small minorities gracefully acquiesce in the face of a sizeable majority, unless that small minority was deemed crucial to the outcome of the report. For example, in 1965, all members of the Wood task force except Budget Director Kermit Gordon and Urban League Director Whitney Young wished to recommend that the Community Action Program (CAP) be shifted from the Office of Economic Opportunity to HUD. Young argued that Negroes greatly distrusted the housing agency and that they would see the transfer of the CAP programs to HUD as an effort to kill CAP. His argument that he could not go back to the Negro community with such a proposal was sufficiently powerful to carry the day.

The role of the staff was likely to vary with the type of task force; the more public and prestigious the task force, the more important the staff became. The staff, under director Howard Moscof, in many ways ran the Kaiser Committee, for instance. As one respondent commented: "The staff set the agenda, wrote the position papers and proposals, and wrote the final report. In a way, the committee had only veto power over the staff."

The 1965 Wood task force staff, directed by Chester Rapkind, on the other hand, performed more in the role of technical back-up, primarily because Wood himself informally played the role of staff director as well as chairman. As he had in 1964, Wood wrote several of the position papers and the final report.

The importance of the staff's role seems to have evolved from the 1964 housing task force experience, in which the task forces were staffed largely by Budget Bureau and agency personnel. Starting in 1965, however, the task forces were provided with professional staffs, selected by and responsible to the White House. It is not too much to suggest that a primary reason the White House moved to professional staffing of outside task forces was to ensure that task forces would respond to Presidential prerogatives, not those of the Budget Bureau (as some claimed the 1964 Wood task force had done) or the agency.

The staff directors maintained a close liaison with the White House staff throughout the deliberations. Thus Moscof of the Kaiser Commission was in frequent communication with the White House through both Fred Bohen and Joseph Califano and was able to exercise some impact on the 1968 Administration proposals through those channels. The White House assigned one of its staff members as liaison to every task force and the liaison often played a major role on those task forces from which immediate legislative proposals were expected. Consequently, Fred Bohen, Califano's assistant, maintained a close liaison with the 1967 interagency task force, sitting in on several of the meetings and representing the President's interest in "thinking big" to members of that group. In 1964, on the other hand, Richard Goodwin was White House liaison to the Wood task force but seldom participated. Harry McPherson played a more vigorous role in the 1965 Wood task force after the White House determined to play a more active role than it had in 1964. The job of the liaison, however, appeared to be less that of acting as Presidential supervisor over the deliberations than that of representing those deliberations to the President himself through Special Assistant Joseph Califano. Califano, who came to the White House in 1965, acted as the President's chief assistant in domestic affairs. He assembled under him a small staff of assistants, one of whom (Fred Bohen) spent the greater part of his time on matters pertaining to housing and urban affairs.[17]

The Budget Bureau, as well as the White House staff, acted as the staff arm of the President, although in a general way distinction can be drawn between their activities. The White House staff took the initiative more in terms of developing new programs and changes of direction, while the Budget Bureau was more active in changing or expanding existing programs. The Budget Bureau was also much more likely to be active in internal task forces than in outside ones. Thus, BOB housing specialist Philip Hanna was quite an active member of the 1967 interagency task force, but the Kaiser Committee had only informal and intermittent contact with BOB. The Budget Bureau played a major role in the 1964 Wood

[17] Before Bohen, Lawrence Levinson performed the same task. In 1966, Milton Semer, former HHFA General Counsel, was the President's resident urban expert and previous to that, Richard Goodwin served in the same capacity both in the Kennedy Administration and in the first years of the Johnson Administration.

task force primarily because Budget Director Kermit Gordon was a member. However, since the 1964 experience, the Budget Bureau's role diminished somewhat as a participant (although key BOB personnel were quite important in terms of evaluating the report). Each task force after 1964 was assigned a BOB liaison whose primary function, according to a White House staff man, was to advise the outside task force of the existence and nature of ongoing federal programs. In addition, the Budget Bureau asked the task force at the end of its considerations to "price out" the cost of the programs it recommends. The task forces were then asked to list priorities in their recommendations if they are restricted to $X$ millions per year, or, alternatively, one-half $X$ millions. The Budget Bureau, as well as HUD, played a significant role in this listing of priorities.

✓HUD itself played a very ambiguous role in task forces. Since the obvious intent of outside task forces was to bypass the Department as a means of policy formulation, HUD officials not only distrusted the outside task forces, but also denigrated their significance. Thus, a HUD official disdainfully observed, "I think the task forces have done an editing job that hasn't been done elsewhere and little more." HHFA itself was represented on the 1964 task force through Assistant Administrator Morton J. Schussheim, who presented the first paper dealing with legislative proposals and who participated quite actively. However, HHFA's negative reaction to many parts of the 1964 report was apparently not appreciated at the White House. In 1965 HHFA was nearly completely bypassed. According to a top HHFA official, Weaver was not even informed that there was to be a task force until the day the White House announced it. An HHFA bureaucrat, on loan from the agency, did a little staff work for the task force, but, unlike the other staff members he was pointedly not allowed to attend any of the meetings.

Three participants of the 1965 Wood task force (Robert Wood, Charles Haar, and William Ross) were appointed to high positions in the newly formed HUD soon after the task force broke up, and that undoubtedly put the Department in better shape so far as relations with the White House were concerned. HUD, as has already been pointed out, dominated the interagency task force the President set up in 1967. Yet, although HUD assigned a liaison to the Kaiser Committee, he did not play an important role in Committee deliberations, nor did HUD do much more than receive criticism from the Douglas Commission.

## Evaluation of Task Force Reports

The evaluation of the task force reports again was a flexible and somewhat unstructured process. The White House received the report and usually sent it to the Budget Bureau for evaluation. The report formally went to the BOB's Office of Legislative Reference, which coordinated the Bureau's review of legislation and policy proposals; but, at least in housing, OLR did not have the expertise to make any real substantive contribution. OLR simply sent the report directly to the Assistant Director in charge of housing (Philip Hanna). However, if the Budget Bureau was deeply involved in task force deliberations (as William Ross of Budget was in 1964 and 1965 and Philip Hanna was in 1967), the evaluation of the report was considerably simplified since it simply occurred as the task force proceeded.

Other interested parties sometimes also got a chance to comment on the report, including the lead agency. However, HUD did not generally play a very significant role in the evaluation process (although the role changed after 1966). In 1964 Richard Goodwin attempted more to do a selling job on HHFA in favor of the major recommendation of the report (rent supplements) than to ask HUD's advice. In 1965, on the other hand, HHFA was completely ignored. The Council of Economic Advisers in particular was sometimes asked to review the report or contribute its own point of view. In 1967, the CEA, for example, studied at the behest of the White House, the structure of the capital market in housing and made suggestions paralleling those of the Kaiser Committee, with respect to the need for improved mechanisms to attract equity capital to the housing market. The CEA, particularly housing expert James S. Duesenberry, was called upon as a matter of course to judge proposed housing legislation with respect to its economic viability and its probable costs and benefits. Use of the CEA's microeconomic judgments on specific policy marked a change from its use almost solely for macroeconomic projections in the late 1940's and 1950's.

The degree of evaluations depended, to some extent, on the closeness with which the White House and Budget Bureau had followed the task force proceedings and on the confidence the President has in the task force. The 1965 Wood task force report, for instance, underwent hardly any review at all. It was taken by White House liaison Harry McPherson directly from Wood, who wrote it, to the President, who approved it. Such cases, however, were the exception rather than the rule. In most instances, there was a review followed by a series of meetings between high-level officials of the institutionalized Presidency. This was the case in 1967 when, according to a participant, Califano, Bohen, Schultze, Hanna, Duesenberry, Weaver, Wood, Moscof, and Treasury Undersecretary Joseph Barr met in Califano's office to hammer out agreement on 1968 Administration proposals.

## Task Forces: How Innovative?

Advocates of the task force process argued that it allowed new ideas to enter the policy process, but many at the same time questioned how innovative the Johnson task forces actually were. As a Budget Bureau official observed, "Task forces fail as innovative forces. Their staffs are not of high quality, because high quality people are not readily available for temporary work. As a result, all they do is pull together existing things instead of coming up with new ideas." A staff member of one of the housing task forces agreed: "The staff basically pulled together ideas that had been circulating. But we did not really come up with any new innovations, nor were we particularly creative."

It does seem true that the task forces which had the greatest immediate impact on legislation recommended programs which were hardly brave new intellectual breakthroughs. HHFA, for instance, had already operated a rent-supplement program on a demonstration basis and the idea had been around for years. As for model cities, which came out of the 1965 Wood task force, a high HHFA official ridiculed its claim to innovation:

The Model Cities approach was on its way to being launched administratively by HHFA even before the task force recommended it. In late 1965, Weaver had selected seven cities and was about to announce them as demonstration cities. This was because Detroit and New Haven had taken advantage of the recently enacted Community Renewal Program to put together an integrated plan for renewing large sections of their cities. We were going to announce the grants when I happened to mention it to McPherson. He talked to the President and then told us to hold it because that was going to be the recommendation of the task force. So it was killed.

Any tendency towards innovation task forces might possess was greatly mitigated by their "representative" membership. Since consensus was the decision-making rule, final agreement was likely to represent not innovative thinking, but compromise between the contending groups represented on the task force. As a high official in the Executive Office of the President admitted, "It is true that with so many interests involved the result is, in some sense, the lowest common denominator."

However, the fact that the task forces did not innovate does not mean that essentially the same course would have been followed had they not been used. Although the ideas may not have been new, they were not yet federal policy, nor, in many cases, were they supported by the bureaucracy. Thus, elements of HHFA opposed the rent-supplement recommendation and HUD was very lukewarm concerning the desirability of attempting to devise any more than a small demonstration city program.

The academic task forces were more often productive in terms of innovative ideas, but they also were often ignored because the ideas were not politically feasible. If any innovation occurred, it was more likely to be in terms of getting new ideas into the thought processes of decision-makers rather than into next year's legislative process. That is, the innovation was more likely to occur over the long run rather than the short run.

Many Johnson Administration officials viewed the task force operation as a significant institutional contribution of the Johnson Administration. However, it is not at all clear that processes within the rubric of Presidential activity are that easily institutionalized, given the highly personalized nature of that office. Each President is likely to create those forms he is most comfortable with. The task force operation was peculiarly suited to the leadership style of Lyndon B. Johnson. It fitted nicely with his oft-repeated emphasis on the need for a partnership between public and private sectors, his lifelong instinct for decision-making on the basis of consensus, and his almost abnormal preoccupation with secrecy.

## Output and Feedback

*Output.* The output of the policy-formulative system in housing policy is, of course, Administration housing proposals. These are not in legislative form, but in program form, and they are usually summarized briefly in the President's State of the Union address before Congress in January. In 1965, the Administration proposed to begin phasing out the 221 (d) (3) program and to replace it with a new rent-supplement program. Although changed drastically by Congress later, the Administration proposal would have aided moderate-income families whose income was too high for public housing and too low for private housing. The occupant would pay 20 percent of his income for rent and the government would pay whatever additional amount was required for the dwelling unit.

In 1966, the Administration proposed a demonstration city program essentially the same in broad scale as what Congress ultimately enacted, although different in some important specifics. The

President in his special message on the cities asked for a coordinated local attack on a blighted area in cities chosen for the program. Cities would put together a coordinated approach consisting of existing federal programs. In addition, they would receive grants up to 80 percent of the local share of those federal programs to be used for any program the city itself wished to devise to attack problems in the chosen area.

In 1967, after hard-fought battles in two successive years, the Administration decided to forego any major proposal. The only program of substance proposed was the $20 million program to eliminate rats in urban areas. In 1968, the Administration proposed a variety of new housing programs, including a low- and moderate-income homeownership plan (236) and an interest subsidy plan (235) designed to replace the 221 (d) (3) program.

*Feedback.* It is much easier to distinguish feedback analytically than it is empirically; empirically feedback tends to merge into system input from the environment. However, it is clear that Administration policy formulation in year $x$ is influenced directly by what happened to Administration policy in year $x-1$. The output, particularly of the substantive legislative subsystem, acts, in effect, as feedback into the policy formulation subsystem. All this merely states the obvious—that those involved in policy formulation base their decisions in part on expectations derived from previous experience. If Administration policy-formulation output does not satisfy the goal of the subsystem,[18] then the subsystem will likely adjust by modifying its output in an appropriate manner the next time around.

[18] In most, but not all, cases the goal is legislative passage. In some cases the goal may be focusing public attention on a problem or satisfying a clientele group or a variety of other possibilities.

# CHAPTER 5

# The Substantive
# Legislative Subsystem

The substantive legislative subsystem, the most open of the four subsystems to inputs from the environment, encompasses that part of the policy process which most political scientists have traditionally studied in legislative case studies, of which Stephen Bailey's *Congress Makes a Law* is probably the best example.[1] Analytically it is useful to divide this subsystem into two further subsystems, one of which is concerned with legislative preparation, the other with legislative consideration and passage.

Legislative preparation includes the shaping of broad statements of intention into specific legislative proposals for Congressional consideration. Although not often viewed as a very significant part of the policy process, participants at this point can have a major influence. As one observer commented: "The broad policy idea is given to the legislative drafter, but the actual way the program will operate depends on the terms of the provisions. These people have a significant impact."

## Legislative Preparation: Environment

The environment at this point in the process consists of the general policy outlines determined at the White House level on the

[1] Stephen Bailey, *Congress Makes a Law* (New York: Columbia University Press, 1950).

one hand and the political atmosphere in Congress on the other hand. The legislative preparation stage seems well insulated from other outside input. The General Counsel's office, despite its clear importance, does not seem to be (or to have been during the Semer era) a focal point for much lobbying activity. Some of the industry groups, particularly those whose own parochial interests could be vitally affected by specific decisions made during legislative preparation, were in contact with the General Counsel's office, but even efforts of these groups were not very intensive. Most lobbying activities aimed at the housing agency, according to observers, were aimed at less insulated and more visible levels of the organization, particularly the Office of the Secretary and the Assistant Secretary (formerly Commissioner) for FHA.

During the period under discussion, after the General Counsel would finish preparing the legislation, it would go back to the Budget Bureau for approval. This stage is the traditional legislative clearance stage of Budget Bureau operations.[2] The legislation would go first to the Bureau's Office of Legislative Review (OLR), a small office which served mostly to coordinate the Bureau's legislative clearance functions.[3] After its review, OLR would then send the legislation to the housing-division examiners.

Bargaining over disputed areas would then ensue between HUD personnel and housing-division examiners. The Budget Bureau, with whom the General Counsel's office worked very closely, protected the Administration's interests while the Department (particularly under General Counsel Milton Semer) tended to concern itself more with what they perceived political realities to be. From all accounts HUD was often politically more cautious than the Administration. Thus both Semer and Secretary Weaver originally op-

[2] See Richard E. Neustadt, "The Presidency and Legislation: Planning the President's Program," *American Political Science Review*, XLIX (1955), 980–1018. Also by Neustadt, "The Presidency and Legislation: The Growth of Central Clearance," *American Political Science Review*, XLVIII (1954), 641–671.

[3] OLR itself often made substantive contributions in some fields if it had the relevant expertise on its small staff, but it does not appear to have had such expertise in housing during the 1960's.

posed the model cities legislation as politically impossible, and they were supported in their opinion by John Barriere, the housing political strategist on the Hill. The Administration, particularly Joseph Califano and Lawrence O'Brien, were much more sanguine about the bill's chances on the Hill. The 1968 interest-subsidy dispute lent further credence to the generalization of HUD's relative caution (see below).

## Legislative Preparation: Conversion Process

Because of their technical skills, lawyers have a major advantage in this part of the policy process. Indeed during the existence of HHFA, the General Counsel's office, under the guidance of Milton Semer and Ashley Foard, played the predominant role in legislative preparation, in collaboration with John Barriere, staff director of the Housing Subcommittee of the House Banking and Currency Committee.

Semer and Barriere approached the legislation with a view toward the political possibilities in Congress, while Foard and his associate Hilbert Fefferman, usually performing the actual task of preparing the bill, supplied technical expertise on behalf of the Agency's own interests. When Semer left after HUD came into being, the power of the General Counsel's office was greatly diminished. Foard and his staff still played a major role in legislative preparation, but they acted more under the guidance of the Secretary's Office, particularly Undersecretary Robert Wood and Deputy Undersecretary William Ross. Furthermore, with Semer's departure the General Counsel ceased to play a dominant role in policy formulation, so that the limits under which the HUD lawyers worked in turning general policy proposals into legislative proposals were more strictly imposed from the outside. Several respondents suggested that the General Counsel's office was intentionally weakened by the HUD reorganization in order to prevent strong challenges to the Secretary's control over his Department. The new General Counsel was a defeated Congressman relatively inexperienced in housing affairs.

In 1968, HUD sent to the Budget Bureau legislation giving a mortgage subsidy to nonprofit cooperative or limited dividend corporations willing to build low- or moderate-income housing. HUD originally suggested that the mortgage be subsidized down to the point where the mortgagee be required to pay only 3 percent and that, in addition, a subsidy in the form of local property tax exemption be included. The Budget Bureau opposed this proposal on the grounds that rents still would not be low enough to attract low-income tenants. Instead, the Bureau suggested a subsidy down to no percent, but without the property tax exemption. HUD opposed this on the grounds of political infeasibility (as an observer explained, "They felt the Hill would view a 0 percent interest as somehow immoral"). The compromise solution was to subsidize down to 1 percent, but with no property tax exemption. Although most of the disputed issues at this stage are incremental in nature such as this was, they are by no means unimportant.

If disagreements persisted, the level of conflict escalated to the HUD Secretary and the Director of the Budget Bureau. Again personality played a major role. The Bureau's hand was undoubtedly strengthened by the fact that all three Budget Directors during the Johnson Administration (Kermit Gordon, Charles Schultze, and Charles Zwick) were economists well acquainted personally with housing policy. The rare deadlocks between Secretary Weaver and the Director, usually highly political in content, then were mediated either by the President himself of his chief assistant, Joseph Califano.

## Legislative Passage: Environment

The second subsystem—legislative consideration and passage—is undoubtedly the most familiar part of the entire policy process. This subsystem is undoubtedly the most open of the four to the environment; yet in many ways it is severely limited by the environment. The openness is understandable for a body which is periodically responsible to the public for return to office. Yet, it is the mood of the constituency itself which serves as one of the limits on the legislative system. If a complex housing program (and very few are not complex) such as rent supplements becomes publicly identified as a form of "socialized housing," there is little Congressmen can do to dispel such a belief even though rent supplement is a program highly praised by the private housing groups.

Part of the reason that it is so difficult to dispel such charges is that Congressmen themselves are not likely to have a good grasp of the legislation. Proficiency in housing legislation demands a knowledge of law, economics, finance, and housing technology which the average person is not likely to have. As a result, housing is an area in which expertise is at a premium. This means that Congressional staff assumes an importance beyond which it usually has when dealing with less complex legislative matters. A former staff assistant commented: "The damn thing is so complicated it's hard to figure out what's even in the bill. This means there are a very few people in Congress who understand what's going on. They have to instead deal with housing in broad policy terms. Do they want more rehab now? If so, give it to the staff and have them work up the techniques which will accomplish it."

Congress is further limited because most legislation, although not all, comes to them from the Administration. The legislature thus does not start from a blank slate, but is put in a position of either voting down, changing, or adding to an already existent set of proposals. Given this limit, it is somewhat surprising to note that Congress often does make extensive substantive changes in housing legislation. In 1965, for example, a middle-income program designed primarily to integrate the suburbs was turned into the low-income, predominantly inner-city, rent-supplement program. The same year Congress wrote a new rent-certificate program into the bill, allowing local authorities to rent existing housing for use as public housing. A year earlier a loan program for rehabilitating slum housing, the first *direct* loan program in the housing area, was successfully added to the Administration bill by Congress, while in 1966 Congress added the 221 (H) program providing 3 percent mortgages for low-income families who wish to purchase housing rehabilitated by a local nonprofit organization. The 221 (H) program, sponsored by Congresswoman Leonor Sullivan (D–Mo.), served as the basis for Senator Percy's homeownership proposal in 1967, and, ultimately, for the Administration's 1968 homeownership proposals. All of these proposals were important; the change to rent supplements, in particular, could be considered redistributive in nature.

The ideological nature of Congress itself clearly limits the options open to the legislative housing subsystem. Each substantive committee considers legislation in the light of what might be acceptable on the floor of Congress, where the level of understanding is on a more general level than in subcommittee, and ideological and partisan considerations are likely to be more prevalent. Thus the more status-quo oriented Congress is, the more difficult it is to pass a redistributive housing bill; the more Republican Congress is, the more difficult it is to pass a Democratic housing bill (and vice versa). The housing subcommittee may therefore shape the bill in order to break down opposition on the floor. In 1966, the Senate Housing Subcommittee added a provision to the model cities bill allowing small communities as well as big cities to be eligible for model cities programs in an attempt to appeal for the votes of Senators from the less urbanized states.

The floor of Congress becomes an especially important part of the environment when the issue is a controversial one. In less controversial matters, bipartisan committee support is likely to mean easy floor passage because members are willing to accept the evaluation of their party's experts on the committee. However, when issues come to the level of public attention, such as rent supplements did, the mood of Congressional constituencies themselves—as perceived by Congressmen—may become a major factor in the environment. Rent supplements was the subject of widespread public debate and controversy, which was carried on in terms of highly emotive symbols such as "socialized housing." In this atmosphere the carefully bargained-for support of Congressman William Widnall (ranking minority member of the Housing Subcommittee) was of little help on the floor, where only twenty-six Republicans supported final passage. So great was the pressure for making rent supplements a party issue that Widnall himself, despite the fact that he had declared himself in support of the entire bill, voted for the earlier recommittal motion which was opposed by only four Republicans.

The importance of the bill to the Administration (clearly an important part of the Congressional environment) also determines the degree to which the White House will involve itself as a direct input on the legislative subsystem. Normally, unless the Administration's prestige is directly committed (as it was, for example, on both rent supplements and model cities), the major role in dealing with the committee is left to the Department itself. When HHFA was in existence, this task was performed mostly through Milton Semer and Ashley Foard in the General Counsel's office. The HHFA Congressional liaison office concerned itself with the more perfunctory function of acting as a service bureau for Congressional requests. However, after the creation of HUD, the Congressional liaison office working in harmony with the Office of the Secretary became the main focus of formulating Congressional strategy, although the General Counsel's office still played a role. Because of their legal expertise, members of the General Counsel's office might be called upon to make quick judgments on proposed changes during committee mark-ups or conference committee. As one respondent observed, "Guys on the legal staff at the proper time can be very important. They may be standing outside the committee room when something important happens and be very influential in shaping that."

Top HUD personnel—usually the Secretary and the various Assistant Secretaries—are of course responsible for testimony before the substantive committees, but committee testimony is not a very important part of the subsystem.[4] One former Congressional staff aide referred to HUD's committee presentations as "nothing but a lot of pageantry."

Whereas good or adequate committee testimony from the Department is not likely to help the legislation very much, it is sometimes alleged that bad testimony can harm it, particularly if it is accompanied by personal animosity. Several respondents suggested that the relations of top HUD personnel in the Johnson Administration with key Hill committees were not the best. One suggested

[4] It is not widely realized that the testimony of any Administration figure must first be cleared through the Budget Bureau for Presidential approval. This can cause some embarrassing moments for an executive who is forced to say in his testimony something he would probably rather leave unsaid. It was suggested that this is what happened to Secretary Weaver when he appeared before the Ribicoff Committee with a statement listing what the Administration's accomplishments had been in dealing with the urban problems which the Committee was studying. The following exchange then occurred, undoubtedly much to the Secretary's discomfiture:

SEN. [ROBERT] KENNEDY: I don't know whether we delude ourselves, Mr. Secretary, just by spending so much time going over what we have done, without really—we wouldn't be holding these hearings and you wouldn't be as concerned as you are if it was not a fact that we are not doing enough.

SECT. WEAVER: I grant that. I said that at the beginning of my statement. But I do think that it is important to indicate where we are and what we have been doing in order to decide where we go from here.

SEN. KENNEDY: It sounds on paper as if the problem is disappearing . . .

SECT. WEAVER: I think you will find that I am not claiming that the problem has disappeared. I think you will find that I am saying that there are things we are proposing to do . . . but I think these all have to be built on the basis of what we have been doing and the experience we have had to date. . . .

SEN. RIBICOFF: I would like to comment, Senator Kennedy, that the listing of all these programs and all the achievements is the greatest argument for the purpose of these hearings to indicate that we have had all these programs and yet we keep slipping further and further behind, and we have reaped and are reaping a whirlwind of violence throughout the nation indicating that our programs have not gone to the heart of the basic problem. . . .

SEN. KENNEDY: . . . as I listen to you talk about the programs, and as I say, I have got the greatest respect for you and I believe you know more about this problem than anyone in the United States, maybe the Chairman's point is correct that perhaps it indicates the need for something different and something new and something that we haven't been doing before, because if this is the answer, we had better get off the ship.

SECT. WEAVER: Let me thank you for your kind remarks . . .

From U. S. Congress, Senate Subcommittee on Executive Reorganization of the Committee on Government Operations, *Hearings, Federal Role in Urban Affairs*, 89th Cong., 2nd Sess. (1966), Part 1, pp. 187–88.

that the rather pedagogical approach characteristic of academics such as Weaver, Wood, and Haar was not well suited for dealing with the Hill. Assistant Secretary Philip Brownstein, who was also Commissioner of FHA, took a different approach, however. While serving as Chief Benefits Director of the Veterans' Administration prior to his appointment to FHA, Brownstein built up a solid constituency on the Hill. In addition, FHA is the most popular component of HUD so far as the Hill is concerned, probably because it has had a wide beneficial impact on large numbers of middle-income constituents. Other participants in committee hearings are not likely to contribute much to the policy process; rather the hearings provide an opportunity for a host of groups, most of them with little influence, to have their day in the sun.

The White House, as has been suggested, becomes involved in behind-the-scenes maneuvers during the subcommittee or committee stage if its prestige is on the line and the bill is in trouble. In such cases it has worked closely with HUD members and key Congressional leadership. This occurred during 1966, for example, when Lawrence O'Brien, Joseph Califano, Weaver, Wood, and Sidney Spector, a new HUD Congressional liaison director, all applied their efforts to lining up sufficient votes to report the model cities bill from the House Housing Subcommittee.[5]

Normally, however, the White House will make its influence felt more on the floor than in committee, through whatever currency of influence it has available with individual members. In both cases there was a fuzzy division of role between Joseph Califano, whose dealings were more concerned with substantive changes in the legislation, and the White House Congressional liaison man (Barefoot Sanders in 1967–68, Lawrence O'Brien previously), who was more concerned with persuading Congressmen to vote with the Administration. The overlap, however, was great, since political strategy often requires substantive changes.

[5] See Robert Semple, "Signing of the Model Cities Bill Ends a Long Struggle to Keep It Alive," New York Times, Nov. 4, 1966, p. 1. for an excellent description of Administration efforts to pass the model cities legislation.

Some groups in the environment also divide themselves according to whether their influence is greater at the committee stage or on the floor. The special-interest industry groups are likely to have a more important impact at the committee stage because they can use their expertise to advantage on matters which affect them but are not perceived to be of great social importance. The mortgage-lending institutions, the realtors, the homebuilders, and the public housing lobby all try to build strong relations with the committees, particularly at the staff level. Groups such as the homebuilders (NAHB), the lending institutions (ABA, MBA, USS & LL), as well as the National League of Cities and Conference of Mayors, also attempt to use their geographical dispersion to the best advantage by bringing members from the Congressional districts of committee members to testify and urge support for the organization's views. The National League of Cities, for example, tries to assure that mayors from the districts of key committee personnel give the League's testimony or at least write or get in touch with the Congressman.

The homebuilders and the mayors groups attempt to exercise an influence (generally, at least during the 1960's, in support of the Administration) on housing policy which has broad social and re-distributive impact. The realtors (NAREB) also are quite active in this sphere, though they were more often opposed to Johnson Administration policy, particularly fair-housing laws. The lending institutions, however, have shied away from larger social issues. As a representative of one of these groups explained, "We don't get into the big social programs. You spread yourself too thin if you do. We're not experts in that kind of thing, so why should we do it. We're experts in our own area."

Nearly all respondents agreed that organized labor was an extremely powerful force on the floor of Congress. Labor is not unconcerned or inactive during committee consideration; but it has a much greater relative impact on the floor, where soliciting support rather than urging substantive changes is of higher importance. Labor's effectiveness stems partly from the fact that its support has helped elect many Congressmen and may well be needed to do so again in the future. Partly, too, its effectiveness stems from the fact that its resources are ample enough to retain a large and skilled staff of Washington operatives, giving it an immense advantage over many other organizations that share a legislative concern in housing.

During the Congressional consideration of model cities in 1966, a loose coalition of groups termed the Urban Alliance emerged. The Urban Alliance apparently was a conscious attempt by HUD to develop a clientele which could support the Department on social issues before Congress. Until 1966, such a clientele did not exist for social issues (except the labor, NAHRO, and National Housing Conference clienteles), although FHA had constructed effective clientele relations with the mortgage-lending institutions for financial issues.[6] As one respondent observed: "HUD has played with its groups only minimally. An intelligent Department would see the League of Cities, Conference of Mayors, NAHRO, and NAHB as natural extensions of itself. Why HUD has not viewed them this way is difficult to say. As a result, HUD is probably more dependent on the support of the President than other Agencies, because they lack other support."

In 1966, the new Congressional liaison director, Sidney Spector, convinced Secretary Weaver to set up a coalition of liberal interest groups which would support HUD. The Alliance was set up under the aegis of the Conference of Mayors and its Director, John Gunther; but HUD for all practical purposes was the motivating force. The Alliance acted as a coordinating device for lobbying, assigning lobbyists of various member organizations to those Congressmen whom it was felt a specific lobbyist could best influence. About seventy-five groups belonged, including such diverse groups as the AFL-CIO, NAHB, the National Council of Churches to the American Hospital Association, Jewish War Veterans, and the Foundation for Cooperative Housing. In return for their aid the

---

[6] Indeed, some question whether the clientele has not controlled FHA for its own interest exists, particularly at local levels.

members were told they would be involved in the policy-formulation process on the social policies they were supporting. Several representatives of member groups complained that this was not the case and that the monthly or semimonthly meetings of the Alliance were usually only strategy sessions.

How important a part do the lobbies play in the legislative subsystem? When the question under consideration is incremental and technical and when social ramifications are either absent or not well publicized, it appears lobbies can make quite effective use of their expertise. Thus, one respondent commented: "During the fifties many of the new legislative programs came into the books via the staffs of the Housing subcommittees, who in turn had been talking to various trade associations and interest groups, particularly NAREB, MBA, NAHB, and USS & LA. These organizations have been particularly effective in developing proposals that would involve their members and address themselves to problems."

However, as redistributive social considerations move into the forefront these groups become much less important, partly because their expertise declines and partly because other elements in the Congressman's environment begin to exercise priority. Thus, nearly every major organization in the housing area supported rent-supplement appropriations in 1967,[7] but the House voted to cut rent supplements completely. The Senate then voted the Administration's full $40 million request and the House-Senate Conference Committee settled on a $10 million appropriation. The House balked at accepting even that amount, finally acquiescing by a vote of 198–184.

Likewise, opposition by one of these groups will not necessarily be sufficient to veto redistributive legislation, as was shown by passage of the 1968 fair housing bill over what appeared to be insuperable obstacles, one of which was NAREB's opposition.

---

[7] Including the homebuilders, the realtors, the mortgage bankers, the mayors, the Negro and civil rights organizations, and, somewhat reluctantly, the public housing officials (National Association of Housing and Redevelopment Officials).

## Legislative Consideration: Conversion Processes

The Housing Subcommittees of the Senate and House Banking and Currency Committees are the focal points in the conversion process. Both subcommittees are relatively autonomous of the full Banking and Currency Committees. Each has its own staff and a budget earmarked specifically for it. Because of this autonomy, subcommittee proceedings assume an importance beyond that which subcommittees normally possess, which of course is not small. The subcommittee chairmen develop, with the aid of their staff, an expertise which the full committee simply cannot match. A Congressional staff member told George Goodwin that, "given an active subcommittee chairman working in a specialized field with a staff of his own, the parent committee can do no more than change the grammar of a subcommittee report." [8] This is a good description of the norm so far as the Housing Subcommittees are concerned.

## Conversion Process: The House

The subcommittee chairman, as this suggests, is the key to the committee's activities. In the House, Albert Rains chaired the subcommittee until 1964, when he retired from Congress. Rains and his staff director, John Barriere, commanded respect from virtually every respondent for their knowledge of housing and their ability to handle legislation. Representative Rains, however, never handled a major redistributive housing bill. His forte was the intricate juggling of interests and bargaining which leaves all concerned satisfied and which is characteristic of incremental "disaggregated" policy.

After Rains retired, William Barrett (D–Penn.) succeeded to the subcommittee chairmanship, but only after vigorous committee infighting. Barrett was a loyal Administration Democrat, but he was

[8] George Goodwin, Jr., "Subcommittees: The Miniature Legislatures of Congress," *American Political Science Review*, LXI (1962), 596.

at loggerheads with Wright Patman (D–Tex.), chairman of the full committee. Patman, according to one account, wished to use the resources of the Housing Subcommittee to aid in his attack on high interest rates and the Federal Reserve System.[9] Thus, he submitted a resolution at the beginning of the Eighty-ninth Congress asking for funds for the full Banking and Currency Committee without requesting separate funds or identity for the Housing Subcommittee. Nineteen members of the full committee, including eight Democrats, immediately submitted resolutions requesting separate funds for the subcommittee. Representatives Patman and Barrett then appeared before the House Administration Accounts Subcommittee, where Patman was asked why a separate resolution had not been submitted. Bruce Norton quotes an Administration Committee member who was present: "It was a messy affair. Patman sat there, right next to Bill Barrett, and proceeded to say that he didn't do it because he didn't have much confidence in his subcommittee chairman! Well, Barrett flared up—the first time I've ever seen Bill get mad—and he asked Patman how he could doubt his ability and competence. Raw nerves were exposed. It was real messy." [10]

Opposition to Patman forced separate funding of the Housing Subcommittee, but it was clear that Barrett's position was not one of strength. There was general agreement that the new subcommittee chairman lacked the technical knowledge and intellectual capacity that Rains had possessed. This was accentuated by the departure of John Barriere, Rains's respected staff director, from the Housing Subcommittee to the Speaker's staff, where Barriere continued to play a major role in formulating housing strategy. Barrett, rather than pursue his own policies, as Rains had done, instead accepted the will of the Administration as his own. As a close observer remarked: "Barrett originates and initiates nothing. His importance is that he acts as a bridge between the Administra-

[9] Bruce Norton, "The Committee on Banking and Currency as a Legislative Subsystem of the House of Representatives," first draft of doctoral dissertation, Syracuse University, 1968, pp. 57–60.
[10] Ibid., p. 59.

tion and Widnall on the one hand, and Widnall and Patman on the other." And as a subcommittee member observed: "The subcommittee is unlikely to make too many changes in Administration proposals except as it is politically necessary to get the bill through. It will accept amendments at the subcommittee if they are not crippling."

The technique the chairman uses to pursue the Administration's ends is the omnibus bill, the traditional vehicle for logrolling—a process whereby support for a piece of legislation is obtained by the simple expedient of allowing each supporter to add his own pet proposal to the legislation (obviously the proposals must not be mutually exclusive if logrolling is to occur). Most housing legislation has been in the form of omnibus bills, and the support of crucial members is enlisted by allowing them to add their own provisions or sweeteners to the bill already before the committee. In this way, controversial issues are muted as much as possible. Thus, in 1966, the Administration agreed to add another $600 million in urban renewal funds to the omnibus bill in order to assuage the fears of some subcommittee members that model cities would cut into urban renewal. The Johnson Administration, through Barrett, played this game particularly well with Representative William Widnall.

As ranking Republican member of the House Banking and Currency Subcommittee on Housing, Widnall was the key Republican force in the House on housing policy. After Barrett's elevation to the subcommittee chairmanship, the New Jersey Republican was, in fact, the driving force behind most changes made in the bill during committee consideration. The Administration, and Barrett as well, appeared to believe that Widnall's support of legislation was necessary both for successful full committee consideration and for victory on the floor. Widnall used this leverage, not to accomplish substantive changes of importance in the Administration bill, but to force the Administration to add to the Administration's omnibus bill programs Widnall himself had developed.

Consequently, in 1965, Widnall bargained with Milton Semer,

John Barriere, and Barrett, and gave his support to rent supplements. But in return, he forced the Administration to accept a leased housing program in public housing.[11] The subcommittee then reported out the bill by a 10-1 vote. Widnall dominated the subcommittee on the G.O.P. side; the minority staff member, Casey Ireland, an employee of Widnall's, worked closely with the majority staff members, Kenneth Burrows and James McEwen. Despite the efforts to work closely with Widnall, however, the atmosphere, according to several respondents, was quite partisan, unlike the Senate subcommittee. The fact that Barrett so transparently represented the Administration undoubtedly encouraged this partisanship.

According to several respondents, Widnall's support assured subcommittee approval and was likely to lessen greatly opposition (and encourage acquiescence) in the full committee, but it meant little on the floor. This was exactly the opposite of the influence Representative Robert Stephens (D–Ga.) seemed to possess. Stephens was viewed by the Administration, along with Widnall, as the key person on the subcommittee. As a moderate Southerner, Stephens was believed to be in a key position to influence large numbers of Southern Democrats, whose support was necessary for legislation and who looked to him as an expert in housing. Thus, it was Stephens who offered the crucial amendment on the floor in the 1965 rent-supplement debate. He asked that the supplement be made available only to those whose income level qualified them for public housing. Originally the Administration bill was aimed at the moderate-level income group above the public housing level. However, judging it impossible to pass any rent-supplement legislation without support of moderate Southerners, the leadership accepted the amendment. Stephens then supported and voted for the legisla-

---

[11] Variously called "rent certificates," "leased housing," or "section 23," Widnall's program has proven one of the most successful HUD runs. Existing housing is rented from private landlords by the local public authority, and the federal government subsidizes the difference between the economic rent and public housing level rent through "rent certificates" paid to the private landlord.

tion, as did forty-one other Southern Democrats. The recommittal motion failed by the slim vote of 208-202.

The remainder of the subcommittee membership had less of an impact than Widnall or Stephens. Democrats Thomas Ashley (D–Ohio), William Moorhead (D–Pa.), and Henry Reuss (D–Wis.) acted as a liberal bloc to expand Administration programs, but they had little success in doing so. In 1967, the trio introduced a bill which would have provided a tenfold increase in the nation's supply of low- and moderate-income housing through extension and expansion of existing urban renewal, nonprofit building and rehabilitation programs, and various FHA insurance programs.[12] The trio, upon occasion, balked at Administration proposals, although White House persuasion usually was effective. Mrs. Sullivan, a St. Louis Democrat, was also basically an Administration supporter with whom the Administration often bargained for her support. Henry Gonzales (D–Tex.) and Fernand St. Germain (D–R. I.), the remaining Democrat members, generally supported the Administration.

On the Republican side, Mrs. Florence Dwyer (R–N.J.) followed Widnall, while Paul Fino (R–N.Y.) was a vocal and sometimes effective critic of HUD's efforts to use housing legislation as a means toward social integration.

The subcommittee as a whole appears to be the most prestigious within the full committee on House Banking and Currency. In 1968, the top eight Democrats in seniority on the full committee comprised the Democratic side of the subcommittee; the top three Republicans in seniority were also on the subcommittee, as were two other Republicans with less seniority. Even with a relatively weak chairman, the subcommittee can have a major effect on important social legislation. Rent supplements in 1965 is certainly instructive here as a case in point. The Administration bill restricted eligible recipients for rent supplements to those with income *above* the level which would make them eligible for public housing. The sub-

[12] "Home Ownership Bills Not Enacted in 1967," *Congressional Quarterly Almanac*, 1967, p. 501.

committee, in response to criticism that rent supplements was a middle-income program from which the needy were being excluded, opened the program to those within the public housing income limits as well. Later, on the floor, the program was *restricted* to those within public housing income.

Subcommittee decisions are usually routinely approved by the full committee. Representative Widnall, often not able to convince his Republican colleagues to support a measure, could sometimes persuade them simply not to vote, or at the least, not to impede the bill's progress. On the floor, Subcommittee Chairman Barrett's inability to handle bills effectively caused problems for the Democrats. Thus, Full Committee Chairman Wright Patman floor-managed the 1968 housing bill after Barrett's less than satisfactory performance with the rent supplement and Model Cities legislation.

Floor strategy was coordinated through John Barriere, former staff director of the Housing Subcommittee under Albert Rains. Barriere since 1965 had been employed in the Speaker's office. The White House, through its legislative liaison, particularly Lawrence O'Brien, played a major and effective role in rounding up votes at the floor stage in both 1965 for rent supplements and in 1966 for model cities. Republicans for their part looked to William Widnall and, to a lesser extent, James Harvey (R–Mich.) for information and cues on complex housing bills, although Widnall, according to several respondents, was not well liked by many of his House colleagues. In cases where technical advice was not necessary because the issue was drawn in redistributive and ideological terms, the Republican Policy Committee or the individual's own judgment was likely to take precedence over Widnall's expertise.

### Conversion Process: The Senate

In the Senate, Senator John Sparkman (D–Ala.) has chaired the Housing Subcommittee of Senate Banking and Currency since 1956. In addition, Sparkman assumed the chairmanship of the full committee upon the defeat of Senator A. Willis Robertson (D–Va.)

in 1966. By virtue of his long involvement with housing legislation and the formal authority derived from his chairmanships, Senator Sparkman was the key figure in housing legislation on the Senate side.

Unlike the House subcommittee, the Senate Housing Subcommittee was run by Sparkman as a bipartisan venture. As a close observer commented, "Sparkman is a consensus man. He likes to present a united front. Thus he gives some influence to people like Senator Tower and Senator Bennett." While the House subcommittee chairman Barrett sometimes accepted amendments and new programs to the Administration bill as a matter of political strategy, Sparkman did so as a matter of personal style. When Senator Percy proposed his homeownership plan in 1967, rather than ignoring it as a Republican proposal, Sparkman scheduled hearings on it and later directed his staff to work out a proposal agreeable to Percy, as well as to Democratic proponents of a homeownership program. In most cases Sparkman made use of the omnibus bill to add distributive changes desired by subcommittee members.

Sparkman utilized Carl Coan, staff director of the Housing Subcommittee, quite extensively. Coan's influence on policy was not insignificant, particularly when Sparkman's own attentions were directed largely elsewhere, as was often the case in the mid-1960's. As one observer remarked: "Coan plays a very significant role. Sparkman is tremendously influential when he wants to be—but of late, he often doesn't want to be. His problem is that he is a Senator from Alabama. He thus stays away from an identification of things helping Negroes."

Until his defeat in 1966, Senator Paul Douglas (D–Ill.) was, next to Sparkman, probably the most important person on the subcommittee. Douglas' representation of liberals on the committee was institutionalized to the extent that the subcommittee allowed Douglas and the liberals one staff man of their own choosing responsible to them. At times, Douglas took leadership of the committee, particularly with issues involving Negroes and civil rights, in which Sparkman, a Southerner, was hesitant to act. The Illinois

Democrat was widely given credit for Senate passage of rent supplements in 1965 under just such circumstances. After Douglas' defeat, the liberal staff member passed into the hands of Senator William Proxmire (D–Wis.), but Proxmire did not take major interest in housing. No other clear liberal leader has emerged, although Senator Edmund Muskie (D–Me.) played a very important role in the model cities legislation in 1966 and Senator Walter Mondale (D–Minn.) was similarly active in 1968.

The ranking subcommittee member, Senator John Tower (R–Tex.) generally opposed redistributive housing programs at their inception as did other subcommittee Republicans through 1966. In 1965 and 1966, the four Republicans on the full committee issued minority reports opposing rent supplements and model cities. In 1965, their report charged that the Administration bill embodied "new and enlarged urban programs bulging with money and power, designed to step up the pace of creeping federalism." [13] Nonetheless, Tower was one of the ten committee members voting in favor of the very bill which the report he signed criticized, an undoubted tribute to Sparkman's ability to get along with his opposite number.

In the Ninetieth Congress, the Republicans added Senator Charles Percy (Ill.) and Senator Edward Brooke (Mass.) to the full committee. Both were moderates and both moved quickly to play a more positive role in committee deliberations than Republicans had previously played. Senator Percy, who was placed on the Housing Subcommittee, introduced his homeownership bill (prepared with the aid of Representative William Widnall), which ultimately resulted in the passage of the Administration-supported homeownership bill. Senator Brooke, though not on the Housing Subcommittee, launched a vigorous attack of FHA and proposed that a new low-income housing division be set up within HUD to handle programs such as rent supplements and 221 (d) (3), which were then administered through FHA. The Ninetieth Congress, in

[13] "Major Housing Legislation Enacted," *Congressional Quarterly Almanac,* 1965, p. 376.

short, marked the end of simple opposition to Democratic proposals by committee Republicans.

In several cases at critical times Senator Edmund Muskie assumed the key role of broker between contending forces. In 1965, Senator Muskie successfully offered an amendment in committee parallel to the amendment Representative Robert Stephens offered on the House floor to change the income limits for rent-supplement recipients, so that they coincided with the public housing limits. In 1966, Muskie and his aide, Donald Nicoll, played the role of intermediary between the White House and the Senate with respect to the model cities bill. According to Robert Semple of The New York Times, after it was determined the bill was in trouble both in the subcommittee and on the floor, a revision was worked out at a series of meetings between Nicoll, Lawrence Levinson (Joseph Califano's assistant), and Philip Hanna of the Bureau of the Budget. Semple reports: "The three went to work immediately. In long late night sessions at the White House, Mr. Nicoll and Mr. Hanna gradually rearranged the criteria (more in form than substance, but the bill was clarified), rewrote the desegregation provision (a politically suicidal element of the bill), and decided to incorporate in the bill provisions for small metropolitan areas." [14]

Both the subcommittee and full committee accepted the revised version of the bill, which Senator Muskie then floor managed. Despite his major role in 1965 and 1966, however, Muskie had little impact either in 1967 or 1968, probably because his interests turned from housing to intergovernmental relations. Once again, it is interesting to speculate on the effect of somewhat random personality variables upon the policy process. Muskie played a key role, not because of his constituency (housing is not a major issue in Maine), nor because his position was one of formal power (he had no formal leadership position on the committee). Rather, his very significant influence was due to the fact that Muskie was well equipped to moderate between the Administration and the committee, primarily because of his own personal attributes and be-

[14] Semple, *op. cit.* (n. 5), p. 1.

cause he happened to be at the right place at the right time. The fact that Muskie did play such a significant role in 1966, but then did not repeat his performance in 1967 and 1968 primarily out of a lack of interest, illustrates the difficulty political scientists face when they attempt to explain policy output entirely in terms of broad societal forces.

Since the Ninetieth Congress, when Senator John Sparkman became chairman of the full committee as well as the Housing Subcommittee, the subcommittee's actions became, in effect, committee actions. This was not always the case under the previous full committee chairman, Senator A. Willis Robertson (D–Va.), an opponent of most government programs. Despite his opposition, Senator Robertson did not try to bottle up new legislation. Changes at the committee level were not uncommon, however. The Muskie amendment to limit rent supplements for those eligible for public housing was a full committee amendment of the subcommittee's bills.

On the floor, Senator Sparkman's leadership, when he was politically able to assert it, was a major asset for bills coming out of the Banking and Currency Committees. As one respondent observed: "Sparkman is very reasonable. He is a liberal on housing matters and yet a real member of the establishment. When a Fulbright or an Ellender comes up to him and asks about something to do with housing, they will believe him. He also has great credibility with Northerners." Primarily because the Senate during the 1960's was much more "liberal" as a body than the House was, the floor stage in the Senate was not an arena for making redistributive changes in housing bills. Rather the tendency was to accept Administration bills put together elsewhere.

However, in contrast to this, the Senate committee and subcommittee stage appears to be a point at which major redistributive decisions may be made. In 1965, Senators Douglas and Muskie brought about the change on income limits of those eligible for rent supplements: a change which was made in the House at the floor stage. In 1966, major changes in model cities were brought about through Muskie's negotiations with the White House described above, and in 1967, the basis of the homeownership bill which became law in 1968 was put together by the Senate committee. The importance of the Senate committee dates from 1965, after the retirement of Representative Albert Rains (D.–Ala.). Prior to that, Rains, as chairman of the Housing Subcommittee in the House, dominated the housing process on the Hill.

## The Conference Committee

According to all reports, Representative Rains dominated the Conference Committees when he was in the House. Since Rains's retirement at the end of the Eighty-eighth Congress, Senator John Sparkman, and Representatives William Widnall and Wright Patman have been the major forces in bringing about agreement between the two branches of Congress. Much of the groundwork—and many of the decisions—of the Conference Committee were set by staff members of the respective subcommittees who maintained a fairly close relationship with each other throughout the year.

One respondent volunteered that the two subcommittees actually operated on a semiexplicit strategy by which each attempted to get the best *possible* bill through its respective chamber, but if a provision was in danger or uncertain in one chamber, it would be dropped and added later in conference if it passed the other. This strategy was based on the fact that conference reports are much less likely to be rejected than original considerations. In 1965, for example, the *Congressional Quarterly* reported:

The Senate July 26 by voice vote and the House July 27 by a 251-168 roll call approved the conference report. . . .

The Senate version of HR 7984 carried an authorization of $7.5 billion for housing programs, while the House bill authorized $6 billion. The wide difference in authorization between the two bills was attributable (in part) to . . . a number of new programs and a broadening of existing ones provided under the Senate bill, but not under the House measure. . . .

The Conference Committee agreed to virtually all the new programs established by the Senate, with only a few minor modifications, and to several other new programs authorized only under the House measure.[15]

## Output

In 1965, Congress enacted the rent-supplement program described on pp. 44–46. Model Cities resulted from the 1966 deliberations as described on pp. 42–43. No major redistributive housing programs were enacted in 1967, although the $20 million rat-extermination program was passed. In 1968, Congress passed a major housing program which included provisions for homeownership for low-income people and mortgage subsidies for low- and moderate-income rental programs.

## Feedback

Because feedback, as has been suggested, is almost impossible to distinguish empirically from input, very little more can be added here that has not been said in previous sections. However, since the participants in the legislative subsystem are relatively constant from year to year, the amount of feedback is clearly high. The experience of previous years is likely to weigh more heavily on the bureaucratic participants whose professional life is dominated by housing than on Congressional influentials, whose memories may be shorter if only because there are so many other things to concern them. HUD can further help to structure feedback so that it is favorable to itself by controlling the flow of information on implementation of recently passed programs; Congress is almost completely dependent upon the Department for information concerning the success of programs with which they have dealt. All this suggests that feedback is somewhat manipulable by HUD and can work in its favor.

[15] *Housing a Nation* (Washington, D.C.: *Congressional Quarterly*, 1966), p. 84.

# CHAPTER 6

# The Appropriations Subsystem

## Redistributive Appropriations vs. Incrementalism

The appropriations subsystem is the most formalized and least open system in the policy process. Its chronological sequences have become institutionalized and most of the roles involved are clearly specified. Because the appropriations process produces outputs which lend themselves to ready manipulation by political scientists (i.e., money, which composes that rarity in social science research, an interval scale), it has been subjected to much more scrutiny by behavioral political science than any other aspects of the policy process save analysis of Congressional roll call voting. Yet, in many ways the appropriations process is also relatively insignificant as far as societal impact is concerned. Aaron Wildavsky writes: "Budgetary calculations are incremental, using a historical base as the point of departure. The existing level of expenditure is largely taken for granted and, for the most part, only small changes are seriously considered." [1]

The process which, as Wildavsky notes, is "incremental," "sequential," "fragmented," and "specialized," [2] normally represents almost the quintessential form of distributive politics. The appropriations subsystem can, however, at times become a major arena for redistributive politics. When it does, it acts "abnormally" ac-

[1] Aaron Wildavsky, *The Politics of the Budgetary Process* (Boston: Little, Brown, 1964), p. 125.
[2] *Ibid.*, Chap. 2.

cording to the description Wildavsky presents. Redistributive politics in the appropriations process are those which determine not simply how much more or less money a program will receive for a given year, but, rather, are those which determine whether that program, if it is perceived as one which redistributes social or economic values from one class of people to another, will continue to exist or whether its funding levels are set at such a low rate that it cannot function effectively. Rather than "normal" appropriations politics, then, this is an extension of the battle fought in the legislative subsystem to a forum where the actors and relative access and influence are quite different.

Redistribution programs quite often shift their focus of battle to the appropriations subsystem for the years immediately after substantive passage. This is exactly what occurred from 1965–68 with rent supplement and model cities. Appropriations battles were not fought over a question of how much money: they were fought over the very existence of the programs. Discussing the rent-supplement appropriations fight in 1967, the Congressional Quarterly commented:

Because the thrust of opposition to supplements has been on the basic concept of the program and not so much on the amount of funds involved, observers believe it unlikely that the Administration could win many additional Senate votes through the ploy of seeking a reduced Appropriation. A spokesman for one special interest group supporting supplements said Republicans were "so determined to beat this program that they'd vote against it if the amount involved was no more than 10 cents." [3]

The following section focuses on the less-studied redistributive processes of the appropriations process, although the more normal processes will also be briefly described.

### Environment

The appropriations subsystem is, of course, limited by the output of the legislative subsystem. It is also limited by the same con-

[3] "Drive Begins to Save Rent Supplement, 'City Funds,'" Congressional Quarterly, July 28, 1967, p. 1317.

straints associated with the mood of the country as reflected in Congress, that are operative upon the legislative subsystem. In addition, the housing appropriations subsystem decision-makers in a broad sense must operate within the bounds of the general performance of the American economy (is it a time for government pump-priming or for restraint?) and competing demands from other governmental subsystems (should money be spent on defense or housing?).

The appropriations subsystem is generally much more insulated from the input of organized environmental groups than is the substantive legislative subsystem. However, when redistributive questions, however disguised, are argued within the appropriations subsystem, the more sophisticated organized groups—particularly the U.S. Conference of Mayors and the AFL-CIO—play a role similar to the one they play in the substantive legislative subsystem. Thus, in 1967, the *Congressional Quarterly* reported:

. . . it was thought the strongest lobbying on the bill was that by big-city mayors in behalf of the model cities plan. Administration sources deemed this support crucial to the salvaging of the Appropriation.

Impetus for the mayors' support came from efforts by the "Urban Alliance"—an ad hoc group of organizations which were generally favorable to Administration housing and urban-aid policies. Organized in the summer of 1966 by representatives of the U.S. Conference of Mayors, the alliance came to include such diverse groups as the AFL-CIO, National League of Cities . . . and a number of other groups.

On May 12—the Friday morning before Tuesday's House debate on the Appropriations bill—the Alliance telegraphed key mayors throughout the nation, urging them to pressure their Representatives to support both the cities and rent supplement plans. A source who participated in the Alliance's discussions told CQ that the mayors had responded with a "massive" lobby effort in behalf of the cities program. . . .[4]

The more public a redistributive appropriations decision becomes, the more groups are likely to become involved. In 1967,

[4] "Lobby Campaign Saves Model Cities Funds in House," *Congressional Quarterly*, June 9, 1967, p. 979.

model cities funds received the public support of a group of twenty-one top businessmen, many of whom had served on earlier Presidential task forces. At the same time local groups and interests, the developing constituency of both rent supplements and model cities, entered the fray. *Congressional Quarterly* observed:

Perhaps the most vigorous lobby effort in behalf of both rent supplements and model cities was that put on by the local civic groups and business interests that stood to gain from the programs. On supplements, this included the local groups that had applied for project sponsorship, the banks which would finance the projects and the construction firms that would put the developments up. On model cities, local support came from civic and service groups, banks, businessmen, builders and other interests that contemplated a role in the projects.[5]

As the above suggests, almost all outside input is concentrated on the Congressional stage of the appropriations process rather than agency or Budget Bureau stages.

## Conversion Process: Budget Bureau and HUD

The appropriations process itself naturally divides into three stages (subsystems, each of them, of the appropriations subsystem). One of these, the Congressional stage, has been exhaustively studied by Richard Fenno,[6] although Fenno concentrates on distributive (the much more common), rather than redistributive appropriations decisions. The other two, the agency stage and the Budget Bureau stage, have been described rather briefly in Aaron Wildavsky's book.[7]

Unlike other subsystems, the appropriations subsystem is highly formalized, although not inflexible. Early in the spring, members of the institutionalized Presidency (Budget Bureau, Council of Economic Advisers, White House staff) meet with economic experts from the Treasury Department and develop a series of economic

---

[5] *Ibid.*, p. 981.
[6] Richard Fenno, *The Power of the Purse* (Boston: Little, Brown and Company, 1966).
[7] Wildavsky, *op. cit.* (n. 1).

assumptions on which the budget will be based. Usually at that point, the departments and agencies are asked to submit preliminary and general estimates of their requirements for the budget year, which will begin on July 1 of the following year. The Budget Bureau provides the departments with the economic assumptions they have developed as guidelines.

HUD responds to the call for a preview by issuing a call of its own to all the Assistant Secretaries and regional administrators asking for estimates of projected new obligational authority, budget expenditures, and program levels. Each HUD Assistant Secretary has his own budget staff, and each works to develop these projections. The Secretary's economist supplies them with a series of assumptions for the coming fiscal year based on the projected state of the mortgage market, homebuilding industry, etc. They are then asked to present a series of figures based on alternative budgetary assumptions. Thus for FY 1969, the assumption was that there were going to be budget cuts. Two alternative constraints were posed to the Assistant Secretaries: (1) no budget-level increases over FY 1968; (2) moderate increases over FY 1968 without expanding the Department's present capabilities. They were asked to submit projections based on both assumptions.

Unlike most years, in 1967 the internal review based on the above assumptions was little more than an academic exercise. The President wished to exert more control than usual over the size of the budget, which he feared would be too high. Thus, he asked the Budget Bureau examiners, rather than the Department itself, to conduct the budgetary preview for FY 1969.

After receiving the preview figures, the President with his economic advisers sketches in the shape of the coming budget. The Budget Bureau, on the advice of the President and White House staff, suggests a planning figure which the Department must try to meet. In late spring and throughout the summer, the Department applies itself to trying to meet that figure. HUD made use of an informal Budget Review Committee (BRC) to accomplish this task. During the latter years of the Johnson Administration, the Committee consisted of Undersecretary Robert Wood, the four program Assistant Secretaries (Philip Brownstein, Charles Haar, Ralph Taylor, and Donald Hummel), Assistant Secretary for Administration Dwight Ink, General Counsel Thomas McGrath, and Deputy Undersecretary William Ross. Although HUD has no centralized budget office (each Assistant Secretary has his own), the Secretary's own Budget Officer (John Frantz) acted as the Executive Secretary and his Budget Office staffed the BRC. Frantz and his staff presented to the BRC their view of what the Department should have and what should be cut to get to the planning figure. This set the basis for the discussion.

Undersecretary Wood chaired the committee, which, as one participant recalled, met nearly twenty times between June and mid-September, 1967. Generally, there was unlimited discussion time; and issues were argued out until a consensus was reached, often on the basis of a good deal of trading and bargaining by the Assistant Secretaries. At times, informal votes were taken. If agreement could not be reached, the final recommendation was left open for the Secretary's own decision. According to this procedure, Wood wrote up the BRC's recommendations and took them to Secretary Weaver, who went over them and decided any unresolved issues. After the Secretary had given his approval, the tentative budget was sent back to the Assistant Secretaries and their budget directors for review and appeal to the Secretary. (Generally the budget must be in the hands of the Budget Bureau by September 30.)

Despite Budget Bureau insistence on development of a program-planning budget system (PPBS), HUD has not enthusiastically adopted this technique. As one HUD respondent commented: "We are not terribly far along in PPB. We observe a lot of the form in the final submission. But the initial submission is done on a conventional basis. Ross's people play with these later and put them into PPB terms just before we sent it off to the Budget Bureau. Congress also insists on getting a conventionally arranged budget."

The Budget Bureau examiners for HUD undertake a comprehensive review of the submitted budget, which includes hearings at which top HUD officials are examined by Budget Bureau housing personnel (Philip Hanna and Donald Kummerfeld during the Johnson administration) and the Assistant Director for the Human Resources Program Division of BOB (William Carey). At these hearings the officials are asked to defend and justify their requests. In November, the Budget Bureau examiners submit their recommendations to the Director, who then meets with them in "Director's Review."

The Director's Review concentrates on major items of Presidential policy. As such, it is likely to be the first opportunity in the appropriations process for major redistributive decisions to be considered. During the Johnson Administration the Budget Directors participated actively and knowledgeably in Director's Review, along with Philip Hanna, the Assistant Division Chief for Housing; William Carey, the head of the Human Resources Program Division, of which the housing division is a part; and Irving Lewis, the Deputy Assistant Director of the Division. Since the last two were not specifically housing experts, most important Budget Bureau housing decisions were the result of collaboration between the Director and Hanna or one of the latter's professional housing experts.

After the decisions are made in "Director's Review," the revised budget is sent back to HUD, where the Secretary goes over it and sends it to the Assistant Secretaries for advice on possible appeals. A respondent involved in the agency–BOB negotiations describes what occurs next: "Around the middle or last half of November, the Secretary will meet with the Director on appeals. On some items the Director may compromise, on others he will hold fast. On some of these Weaver may say, 'I am going to appeal to the President.' Some of these issues simply go to the White House staff level, to Califano, where they are solved. Others go directly to the President for decision."

The process described above is routine, but apparently well insulated from outside pressures. It is only when appropriations reach the Congressional level that much lobbying occurs. The Budget Bureau, however, disappears as an important force when the focus switches to Congress. HUD carries its own ball during the Congressional appropriations process, although it receives needed aid from the White House if the latter's prestige is on the line—as it was in both 1966 and 1967 with rent supplements.

### Conversion Process: The House

The HUD appropriations are first considered by the Independent Offices and Department of Housing and Urban Development Subcommittee of the House Appropriations Committee. The very process of selecting members for the Appropriations Committee ensures that the committee is likely to be more conservative than the House as a whole, since the process emphasizes "legislative responsibility" and favors those from "safe districts." [8]

On the Appropriations Committee itself, in the Ninetieth Congress, 59 percent of the members came from primarily rural or small town districts, as compared to 51 percent in the entire House. More importantly, on the Independent Offices Subcommittee, which handles all the HUD appropriations—the major subcommittee handling urban affairs—six of the ten members were from primarily rural or small town districts, three from primarily suburban districts, and only one, Representative Edward Boland (D–Mass.) from a primarily urban district. Boland was the subcommittee member who pushed HUD's needs before the subcommittee and whom HUD, according to several respondents, felt easiest in working with. In addition, the full committee chairman and ranking minority member each have and often exercise, an ex-officio vote on the subcommittee; during the Eighty-ninth and Ninetieth Congress, Representative George Mahon (D) representing a rural Texas district, was chairman and Representative Frank Bow

---

[8] Nicholas A. Masters, "Committee Assignments," *New Perspectives on the House of Representatives,* eds. Robert Peabody and Nelson Polsby (Chicago: Rand McNally, 1963), pp. 47–49.

(R–Ohio) from suburban Cleveland, was ranking minority member. Partly because the subcommittee chairman was new, most respondents reported that Representative Mahon played a major role on the subcommittee.

The chairman of the subcommittee, Representative Joseph Evins (D–Tenn.) had succeeded to that position upon the death of former Subcommittee Chairman, Albert Thomas (D–Tex.). After assiduous effort by HUD and Administration officials, Evins, by the end of the Johnson Administration, could be counted upon as a safe vote for city programs. Normally, support of the Appropriations Subcommittee chairman would assure success for a department. Fenno reports that "Committee members are in unanimous agreement that the subcommittee chairman is the most influential decision-maker within this group." [9] However, where redistributive issues are concerned, the support of the subcommittee chairman may not be enough. Thus, in 1967, a fierce fight ensued in the subcommittee over model cities funds, despite Chairman Evins' support. The subcommittee first rejected, eight to four, a proposal to approve the entire $662 million allotment the Administration had requested. Then, by the narrowest of margins (a six-to-six tie) the subcommittee declined to knock out all the money except $12 million in planning funds. According to the *Congressional Quarterly*, the vote split as follows:

*For eliminating money:*
 Chairman Mahon (D–Texas)
 Rep. Marsh (D–Va.)
 Rep. Bow (ranking committee minority member) (R–O.)
 Rep. Jonas (ranking subcommittee minority member) (R–N.C.)
 Rep. Minshall (R–O.)
 Rep. Talcott (R–Cal.)
*For retaining money:*
 Rep. Evins (Subcommittee Chairman) (D–Tenn.)
 Rep. Boland (D–Mass.)

[9] Fenno, *op. cit.* (n. 6), p. 169.

Rep. Shipley (D–Ill.)
Rep. Giamo (D–Conn.)
Rep. Pryor (D–Ark.)
Rep. Wyman (R–N.H.) [10]

The subcommittee then unanimously voted to allot $237 million to Model Cities. This very brief discussion of one redistributive case is instructive because it points out clearly how great a difference there is between this and the "normal" distributive appropriations process described by Richard Fenno. Fenno observes that in appropriations subcommittees "the pervasiveness of such norms as reciprocity, compromise, and minimal partisanship help to meet House expectations that consensus-building procedures be followed." [11] Yet, in the case just discussed in which the very existence of a broad social program was at stake, the norms Fenno describes either broke down completely or wilted badly in the heat of battle.

The full committee usually routinely accepts the subcommittee recommendation. However, on redistributive issues this may not always be the case, particularly when the subcommittee membership characteristics differ markedly from those of the full committee. In 1966, the Subcommittee consisted of three Northern Democrats and a liberal Southerner (Subcommittee Chairman Evins), plus three Republicans. It reported out $20 million of the Administration's $35 million request for rent supplements. However, the full committee, which despite its overwhelming thirty-four to sixteen Democratic majority, had fifteen Southern or Border Democrats on it, voted twenty-five to twenty-one to throw out the entire rent-supplement appropriation.

The House Appropriations Committee's recommendations normally are ratified with ease on the House floor. The Committee succeeds, according to Fenno, primarily because it is able to maintain a very high degree of unity on the floor: "Finally, and most

[10] "Lobby Campaign . . . ," *op. cit.* (n. 4), p. 980.
[11] *Ibid.*, p. 189.

important, the Committee succeeds on the House floor because it usually maintains a high degree of unity. . . . The extraordinary effort at internal integration, especially at minimizing partisanship, brings success to the floor." [12]

But, a look at some redistributive decisions again suggests that Fenno's generalizations apply mainly to ordinary distributive decision on which unity is rather easy to achieve. Thus, in the battle over rent supplements just discussed, the full committee's recommendation to cut all rent-supplement funds was overturned on the floor, 192-188. The floor amendment, reinstating the $20 million the subcommittee had originally provided, was offered by Representative Boland, a member of the subcommittee. On the vote, all four Democratic members of the subcommittee were recorded in favor of Boland's amendment; all three Republicans were opposed. In all, the Democratic members of the committee split twenty-one to thirteen in favor of reinstating the rent-supplement appropriation, while all sixteen Republicans voted or were announced in opposition.

Similarly, in 1967, the subcommittee reduced the Administration's $40 million rent supplement to a rather token $10 million. However, when the bill came to the floor, Representative Glenn Davis (R–Wis.), a member of the committee, moved to delete all rent-supplement money, thus killing the program. Again, the move was opposed by both Chairman Mahon and Subcommittee Chairman Evins, but was formally backed by the House Republican leadership. Republicans on the Appropriations Committee voted unanimously for the deletion, including the four G.O.P. members of the subcommittee. Democrats on the Committee opposed the amendment by a vote of twenty-two to five. All five who favored were from the South; one of the five was on the subcommittee.

In the same year, the subcommittee's decision, after much strife, to give $237 million for model cities [13] was challenged on the floor by Representative Robert Michel (R–Ill.), a member of the full

[12] *Ibid.*, p. 500.
[13] *Ibid.*, p. 257.

committee who moved to knock out the entire appropriation except $12 million in planning funds. Both Chairman Mahon and Subcommittee Chairman Evins opposed the motion. The Republican party leadership, however, went on record as being in favor of the cut. Republicans on the committee then voted eleven to six in favor of the cut, with three of the four G.O.P. subcommittee members voting against their own subcommittee recommendation. Democrats on the committee opposed the cut by a twenty to eight vote; one Southern Democratic subcommittee member voted in favor. The amendment was rejected 213-193.

The above suggests not simply an aberration, but a pattern which existed for redistributive housing appropriations decisions throughout the period studied.[14] Committee proceedings were partisan and divisive rather than nonpartisan and consensual; so were subcommittee deliberations to a somewhat lesser extent. The reason for this, as well as for the floor battles, was that major redistributive battles (rent supplements and model cities) already fought once through the substantive legislative system, were being refought in a different arena. In this new arena, lineup of forces was more favorable, at least in committee stage, to opponents.

## Conversion Process: The Senate

The Senate Appropriations Committee is viewed, and views itself, as a board of appeals. The House cuts the budget; the Senate judiciously restores some of these cuts. As Richard Fenno observes:

As Senate Committee members view it, their primary goal is to listen to and act on appeals brought to them by people who are dissatisfied with the appropriation bill passed by the House. These people normally include executive agencies, clientele groups supporting such agencies, members of the House and members of the Senate. Committee members

---

[14] The first attempt at funding rent supplements was defeated by the House in 1965; even as late as 1968, appropriations to keep the program *functioning* were a major legislative struggle.

describe themselves variously as a "court of appeals," "appellate court," "appeals court," and "court of last resort." [15]

Since, in recent years, the Senate has been more "liberal" than the House, the Senate Appropriation Committee's norm of restoring some House cuts has been reenforced, particularly on redistributive decisions. In 1967, for example, the committee restored $300 million of the $425 million the House had cut from the model cities appropriations HUD had requested and all $40 million from the requested rent-supplement appropriation.

The Senate Subcommittee on Independent Offices handles the HUD appropriations. In both House and Senate, the fact that HUD appropriations are handled by the Independent Offices Subcommittee is a holdover from the HHFA days when the housing agency was *indeed* an independent office. Efforts to create urban affairs subcommittees have failed, at least up until 1969, as members of the Independent Offices Subcommittee have zealously guarded what they consider to be part of their own domain. One by-product of this anachronism is that both "urban" subcommittees are overloaded with rural members. In the Senate, of the nine Democrats and seven Republicans on the subcommittee, in the Ninetieth Congress, only four can be considered to come from urban states—Warren Magnuson (D–Wash.), John Pastore (D–R.I.), Clifford Case (R–N.J.), and Jacob Javits (R–N.Y.).

Subcommittee Chairman Magnuson was, according to respondents, a strong chairman who was very favorable to Administration appeals. Ranking minority member Gordon Allot (R.–Col.) was the most important Republican and could be persuaded to support the Administration—in 1967, for example, he voted in subcommittee for the rent-supplement appropriation. Senator Pastore (D–R.I.) was likely to be the most persistent and effective member of the Senate at arguing the Administration's case. Perhaps the crucial subcommittee member, though, was Senator Allen Ellender

[15] "Lobby Campaign . . . ," *op. cit.* (n. 4), p. 537.

(D–La.). Ellender, who was one of the original sponsors of public housing, stood as the swing vote on a subcommittee in which five of the nine Democrats were Southerners. In 1967, for example, he cast the deciding vote in favor of rent supplements. However, he did so only after insisting that language be written into the Appropriation bill's report ensuring that nonprofit sponsors who make use of FNMA special assistance funds must put up an equity investment of at least 5 percent. This provision was heatedly debated on the floor and several Senators, including Senator John Sparkman, Chairman of the Banking and Currency Committee, urged that HUD ignore the provision since a committee report has no formal legal standing. However, Senator Magnuson, although announcing he had personally opposed the recommendation, emphasized he had to accept it in the report in order to obtain sufficient votes to gain approval for the rent-supplement funds. He advocated that the report be heeded or future HUD appropriations might be greatly endangered.[16]

Partly because of the makeup, there was not nearly as much partisanship on the Senate Appropriations Subcommittee on Independent Offices as in the corresponding House subcommittee. Three of the seven G.O.P. subcommittee members—Javits, Case, and Smith (Me.)—were from the "moderate-liberal" wing of the Republican Party and either quite favorable or not predisposed against Administration requests on housing. The Senate subcommittee was also more autonomous than the House subcommittee, since Senate Appropriations Chairman Carl Hayden (D–Ariz.) did not take an active interest in its affairs as Chairman George Mahon did in the parallel committee in the House.

The Senate floor, at least during the 1960's, was much more friendly to HUD appropriations than was the House floor. In 1967, for example, the Senate defeated by a vote of 56-33 an amendment to reduce rent-supplement funds from $40 million to $20 million. The House had previously knocked out all rent-supplement funds

---

[16] U.S., *Congressional Record*, 90th Cong., 1st Sess. (1967), September 20, 1967, S13342-44.

by a vote of 232-171.

The Conference committees were apparently dominated by Representative Mahon and Senator Magnuson, with Senator Ellender playing a very important role as a swing vote.

The Administration relied mostly on HUD itself to push appropriations measures through Congress. The Budget Bureau stayed away from Congressional appropriation politics and the President or his legislative liaison personnel became active only when an important Administration-backed program—usually a redistributive one such as rent supplements—was in danger. If he did become active, the President was likely to concentrate on rounding up floor votes, leaving the more delicate negotiations with committee members to HUD. Inside HUD, the Congressional liaison office spearheaded the appropriations lobbying effort. The Congressional liaison office, headed by Sidney Spector from 1965–67 and Edward Lashman thereafter, played a more effective role in appropriations than it did in substantive legislation, since simply money rather than the incredible complexities of housing legislation was involved.

HUD is not without effective resources to influence Congressional consideration of its appropriations. It can utilize output from the operational subsystem to threaten reward or punishment of Congressmen, as it did with model cities funds in 1967, for example. The list of cities to be chosen for the grants was not issued until November 16, 1967, a delay of about four and a half months from when it was originally scheduled to be announced. The model cities appropriations had finally been approved by the House on October 26, a short three weeks previous to the announcement. Although it is possible that HUD delayed the announcement more out of fear of losing the votes of representatives from unsuccessful applicant cities than from any intention to positively award those Congressmen who voted favorably, it is nonetheless interesting to look at the distribution of the grants. Overall sixty-three cities received grants out of approximately 200 applicants. About half of the Congressmen whose districts included applicant cities saw at least one city in their district awarded money. Yet, six of the seven members of the House Independent Offices Subcommittee whose districts included or were encompassed in applicant cities received the grants. These were:

Smithville, Tenn.—represented by Subcommittee Chairman Joseph Evins, a supporter of model cities.

Texarkana, Ark.—represented by Rep. David Pryor, a key vote for model cities in the subcommittee where efforts to cut it had failed by a six to six vote.

Manchester, N.H.—represented by Rep. Louis Wyman, a Republican who was the lone Republican supporter of the appropriations.

Charlotte, N.C.—represented by Rep. Charles Jonas, ranking minority member who opposed the appropriations.

New Haven, Conn.—represented by Rep. Robert Giamo, a supporter of model cities.

Springfield, Mass.—represented by Rep. Boland, a supporter of model cities.

It seems fair to speculate that HUD was making attempts to build support for future model cities appropriations, attempts which at the same time involved rewarding some key members for their support in anticipation of receiving a grant. An Administration spokesman observed that the main immediate goal so far as model cities was concerned was to develop a constituency for it in order to assure favorable Congressional consideration for appropriations. The first list of model cities winners seemed well structured to accomplish that. In early 1968 another smaller list of grants was announced well before the 1968 appropriations fight.

Other output from the operational subsystem proved less happy for HUD. A set of guidelines issued a month before the vote on rent supplements in 1965 announced in the first paragraph: "Important criteria with regard to approval of a rent supplement project will include full consideration of its contribution to assisting in integrating income groups and furthering the legal requirements and objectives of equal opportunity in housing." [17] The resulting Congressional uproar made the appropriations outlook very dim indeed, and the guidelines were promptly withdrawn. The new guidelines, however, were vigorously attacked on the floor by Representative James Harvey (R–Mich.), a member of the Housing Subcommittee of Banking and Currency. Harvey claimed that under the guidelines families with assets of up to $25,000 would be eligible for rent supplements, and he urged that the appropriation for the program be defeated. Administration supporters were unable to show that Harvey was incorrect and the appropriation was defeated 185-162. The guidelines were changed to meet Harvey's objections by 1966.

Redistributive politics sometimes enters the appropriations process through substantive riders to appropriations bills, a supposedly illegal, but nonetheless much employed device. The case of the local veto in rent supplements was perhaps the most important. Originally the rent-supplement program was to operate simply through the private market in the same way as any rental development. This provided obvious opportunities for integrating the suburbs through private nonprofit developers building rent-supplement apartments in those areas. However, in 1966 House Independent Offices Subcommittee Chairman Joseph Evins offered a rider to the HUD appropriations which limited rent-supplement projects either to those cities with workable programs or to cities in which the projects were specifically approved by the local governing body. Representative Evins explained that he offered the rider to pick up the Southern votes which were necessary if the appropriation was to pass at all, "to make the impossible possible . . . to get the program approved." [18] The rider was opposed by Representative William Fitts Ryan (D–N.Y.) on the House floor during debate. Ryan complained that the limitation "clearly . . .

[17] "Rent Supplement Program Package" Federal Housing Administration MF Letter No. 63, September 28, 1965.
[18] "Restricted Rent Supplements Funded by Bare Margin," *Congressional Quarterly Almanac*, 1966, p. 245.

has been written into the bill to block the possible exodus of low-income families into communities outside the central core of our cities. Local officials in these lily white bedroom suburbs can be expected to exercise this veto power to prevent the have-nots from coming into the community with the haves." [19] Nevertheless, the local control rider was adopted.

Table 3. HUD Appropriations, 1966–68 (in millions)

| Fiscal year | Requests | Final |
|---|---|---|
| 1966 | $2,683 | $2,651 |
| 1967 | 1,611 | 1,499 |
| 1968 | 2,561 | 1,948 |
| 1969 | | |

NOTE: In important redistributive issues such as rent supplements and model cities, appropriations outputs are not nearly so predictable, and cuts may be much more severe. (See Table 4.)
SOURCES: The Budget of the United States Government, Fiscal Years 1967, 1968, 1969, and 1970.

Table 4. Rent Supplement and
Model Cities Appropriations, 1966–69 (in millions)

| Fiscal year | Rent supplement | | Model cities | |
|---|---|---|---|---|
| | Request | Final | Request | Final |
| 1966—1st supplemental | $30 | $ 0 | $ | $ |
| 1966—2nd supplemental | 30 | 12 | | |
| 1967 | 35 | 20 | 12 | 11 |
| 1968 | 40 | 10 | 662 | 312 |
| 1969 | 65 | 12 | 1,000 | 625 |

SOURCES: See "Sources" for Table 3.

[19] U.S., Congressional Record, 89th Cong., 2nd Sess. (1966), March 29, 1966, p. H7116.

## Output and Feedback

The output from the appropriations subsystem is easily measured in terms of dollars. As is the case with nearly all agencies, the HUD budget is usually less than what the Administration requests, but not drastically so. (See Table 3.)

# CHAPTER 7

# Guidelines and Operation

## Why Are Guidelines and Regulations Important?

The processes by which administrative agencies devise guidelines and criteria for the operation of programs passed and funded by Congress have been almost totally ignored by political scientists. This is so despite the fact that important decisions, including some that are manifestly redistributive, often occur at this stage in the policy process. Thus, on June 2, 1967, HUD issued guidelines which specified that first priority should be given to those urban renewal projects which would directly aid large numbers of low-income people to obtain decent jobs and housing. The trend in urban renewal previously had been to clear slums and replace them with more profitable middle- and upper-income housing. Similarly, on August 2, 1967, FHA changed its guidelines so that loans could be granted if they were found to be of "acceptable risks" rather than "economically sound," as the previous criterion had specified. The "economic soundness" criterion had assured that most FHA mortgages were granted to moderate-income people and above rather than low-income people.

Despite the lack of attention this process has received from political scientists, it is a relatively open subsystem. Many organized groups recognize the importance of these guidelines and strive to shape the regulations so that they are as favorable as possible to their own interests. At the same time, efforts to gain control of the various programs sometimes precipitate vigorous fights both within and without the agency in question. Thus, the Public Housing Administration of HHFA tried without success to gain administrative control of the rent-supplement program—a program which it saw as potentially dangerous to the whole concept of public housing. It was aided in its efforts by NAHRO, the professional organization of local public housing administrators. However, unlike Congressional activity and, to some extent, policy formulation —both of which occur at relatively discrete points in time—the operations process is a continual one. Perhaps it is for that reason that this part of the policy process has been ignored so unjustifiably.

## Environment

The environment provides the operations subsystem with strict constraints—the provisions of the legislation passed by Congress. As a participant in the drawing up of the model cities guidelines observed, "We took our basic cues from what Congress had specified in the bill. That was the rock on which the temple was built." Moreover, the members of the subsystem must consider future relations with both the substantive legislative committees and the relevant appropriations subcommittees. Any breaches of Congressional intent which are detected [1] could easily result in future action detrimental to the agency. For example, in 1965, as previously mentioned, Representative James Harvey (R–Mich.) argued that the rent-supplement guidelines clearly flouted Congressional intent to limit the program to low-income families since it permitted some families with assets up to $25,000 to be eligible participants.

---

[1] Most such breaches are of the spirit, not the letter of the law. And not all are detected. Thus, a provision in the 1965 Housing bill—the Widnall Leased Housing Plan—specified that existing private housing could be rented as public housing by public housing authorities. An alert member of HUD's Office of the General Counsel argued successfully within HUD that newly constructed houses could be eligible for this program because, once a house was built, it was existing. The ruse, according to a member of the General Counsel's office, has been completely successful.

Citing the guidelines, Harvey led a successful fight to deny the program its initial appropriations.

External events may also set the tone, if not determine the results of the operations process. The riots in 1967 in Cincinnati, Newark, Plainfield, and Detroit precipitated a series of major changes in HUD guidelines on citizen participation, relocation policy, and FHA loans to low-income areas. Included in these were FHA's change to an "acceptable risk policy" and its announcement of a free housing counseling service for prospective home-seekers. A HUD official described a series of meetings to change the guidelines as "a direct result of the riots." He contended, however, that the riots merely accelerated the change of pace which would ultimately have occurred anyhow.

The more sophisticated organized groups expend major efforts to influence the guidelines. The financial groups, because of their close relationship to FHA, have been particularly effective at this point, as has NAHRO with urban renewal and public housing, and the mayor's organizations with urban renewal. Thus, as a representative of the Mortgage Bankers Association observed, "I spend the bulk of my time on FHA and VA day to day ongoing programs as well as on legislation." And, as a NAHRO representative commented, "Our people represent local experience. HUD sees us to some extent as part of its constituency. We have a role both in developing administrative criteria and in program development." On the other hand, a few organizations, particularly NAREB, were notably ineffective at this stage. Because of their staunch opposition to open housing, NAREB was reputedly persona non grata with Secretary Robert Weaver for several years. A NAREB official himself lamented, "The lobbying we do is exclusively with Congress; there is nothing we can do with the agency."

Members of Congress can at times also exert a direct influence. During the latter half of 1967 Senator Edward Brooke (R–Mass.) directed a series of attacks at FHA for its lack of social concern. Senator Brooke suggested that programs affecting low-income people be transferred out of FHA and into a new office for low-income housing. The Senator's attack was cited by HUD respondents as a major cause for FHA Commissioner Philip Brownstein's shape-up-or-else speech to field office directors in October, 1967. Brownstein outlined the social problems facing cities and then warned his underlings: "If FHA fails to respond effectively and affirmatively to this challenge, if FHA fails to produce the results needed, then no longer will FHA be looked upon as our nation's housing agency." [2]

The attack on the 1965 rent-supplement preliminary guidelines is an outstanding example of the way in which Congress can exert influence in this area. Immediately after passage of the program, but prior to the attempt to achieve a small beginning supplemental appropriation, HHFA produced a series of preliminary guidelines. The second sentence of these guidelines reads, "Important criteria with regard to approval of a rent-supplement project will include full consideration of its contribution to assisting in integrating income groups and furthering the legal requirements and objectives of equal opportunity in housing." [3]

Immediately, Representative Paul Fino (R–N.Y.) renewed the attack he had made earlier, claiming that the guidelines proved HHFA was more interested in social engineering than in housing poor people.[4] Southern Democrats, many of whom had voted for the original program, now began backing off. Forty-one of ninety-two Southern Democrats had voted for the original authorization; only nineteen of eighty-one voted for the appropriations.

The appropriations were defeated by twenty-three votes, and, according to several close observers and participants, the integration specter, although not clearly articulated publicly, was the major weapon used against the funding. The revised rent-supplement guidelines omitted all mention of the integration criteria. But just to make sure, the Appropriations Committee in 1966 added the

[2] "Riots, Rebuke Forcing FHA to Fill Needs of Poor, Slums," *HUD Clip Sheet*, November 13, 1967, p. 8.
[3] "Rent Supplement Program Package," Federal Housing Administration MF Letter No. 63, September 28, 1965.
[4] U.S., *Congressional Record*, 89th Cong., 1st Sess. (1965), October 14, 1966, p. 26988.

requirement that only communities with workable programs could be eligible for rent-supplement funds, thus ensuring that communities that did not wish Negroes in their midst could prevent that result, simply by refusing to draw up a workable program.

Because they review housing programs annually, the appropriations subcommittees are likely to provide much greater input into the operations subsystem than do the substantive committees. The Government Operations Committee may also become involved when its curiosity is piqued. Such involvement is viewed with much trepidation by HUD employees since the committee has never been very sympathetic towards social programs.[5]

## Conversion Process: The Administration of HUD

The reorganization of HHFA into HUD in 1965 produced major changes in the influence pattern within the organization. Prior to the advent of the Department, the housing agency had consisted of several semi-independent agencies. A particularly important policy difference arose between William Slayton, the strong-minded Commissioner of the Urban Renewal Administration, and Robert Weaver, then Administrator of HHFA. Weaver, according to a HUD official involved, wanted urban renewal to be directed toward housing low- and moderate-income people, whereas Slayton thought this was economically infeasible because it did not provide sufficient profit incentive to private enterprise. Slayton triumphed and, as a result, urban renewal for several years following 1961 continued primarily as a program which tore down slums and erected in their place middle- and upper-income housing.

FHA at the same time remained the most independent of the autonomous agencies. Its powerful clientele groups (the homebuilders and the mortgage bankers) and its independent statutory existence

[5] An exception was the Ribicoff Committee's hearings on cities, which dramatized the fact that government was not doing enough to solve urban problems. The Ribicoff Committee was a subcommittee (on Executive Reorganization) of the Government Operations Committee.

allowed the agency, particularly at its lower levels, to flout the Administrator regularly. Because of the nature of these clientele groups, FHA tended to pursue a more conservative course than the rest of HHFA. It had a built-in conflict with the Urban Renewal Administration, since, even though FHA loans in urban renewal areas were granted on the criterion of acceptable risk rather than economic soundness this criterion was subject to a narrower interpretation by FHA than by Urban Renewal. As a result, developers were often unable to secure FHA loans for urban renewal areas.

The Public Housing Agency depended on NAHRO as its main clientele group. However, during the last years of HHFA, PHA was administering a debilitated program. Finding it impossible to acquire sites for public housing, PHA tried unsuccessfully to convince the Urban Renewal Agency to build public housing in renewal areas. The public housing people also vigorously opposed the rent-supplement program, which they perceived as a threat to their entire existence.

Although this kind of conflict did not totally disappear, the reorganization of HHFA into HUD changed this situation by centralizing all the agencies under the authority of the Secretary.[6] Urban renewal and public housing were combined into a single unit, under an Assistant Secretary for Housing and Renewal Assistance. William Slayton left and the new Assistant Secretary, Donald Hummel, was reportedly not a man of strong independent views. It was clear that urban renewal had been downgraded in favor of the new Model Cities Administration. As a bitter adherent of urban renewal observed: "A large part of the reorganization was aimed at tearing the Urban Renewal Agency apart. It had developed a reputation of trying for autonomy like FHA and of operating independently. The reorganization was partly vindictive. Model cities is now the Administration's great hope."

At the same time Secretary Weaver successfully downgraded the

---

[6] FHA retained its existence as an independent entity because of the insistence of powerful clientele groups in the financial community who transmitted their concern to the Hill.

General Counsel's office which, as has been noted, maintained a strong voice on all major policy questions. Milton Semer left and Weaver did not appoint a new General Counsel for nearly a year. Finally, the Secretary appointed Thomas McGrath, a defeated New Jersey Congressman, as General Counsel. McGrath, according to all respondents, was mostly a figurehead who, because of his lack of expertise, was not able to play a major role. Ashley Foard, a career civil servant loyal to Weaver who had been Acting General Counsel during the interregnum, continued to perform as de facto General Counsel.

Weaver further consolidated control in the Secretary's office by utilizing Undersecretary Robert Wood for many administrative tasks that had previously devolved upon the autonomous agencies. Decisions were funneled to the Secretary through Wood and Deputy Undersecretary William Ross. Despite his rather clouded public image as a "weak" Administrator, there was unanimous agreement of those interviewed within HUD that it was Secretary Weaver who made the major decisions within the Department and made them stick. This control was as firm in issuing guidelines as on other policy matters. As a participant observed, "Weaver has the effective last say on guidelines. Nobody would think to issue something without his approval."

Weaver was able to exert control largely because the expertise he possessed enabled him to keep on top of the Department's programs. Respondents were in nearly unanimous agreement that although the Secretary's preferred style was no more one of cautious conciliation than of leadership, he was clearly the top decision-maker in HUD.

### Conversion Process: Guideline Preparation

The drafts of regulations are generally the responsibility of program administrators in each office, but they are likely to receive general direction from the General Counsel's office. A participant responded: "Who will be involved in writing these things? Lawyers for sure, even though the actual writing may fall to people in program administration. But they are dependent on material from the General Counsel's office, which was responsible for the wording in the legislative proposals plus all the backup work for the Budget Bureau, the substantive committee, and the Appropriations Committee."

The General Counsel's office, in short, has the greatest acquaintance with both the language and intent of the legislation. In some cases it may even have written the report. Not only does it provide the material, but it reviews and approves drafts of guidelines. During the Johnson administration, Ashley Foard, Hilbert Fefferman, and Irving Margulies were the major forces at work within the General Counsel's office on this.

In FHA, Carter McFarland, Assistant Secretary Philip Brownstein's idea man, was most responsible for coming up with the initial proposals for new or changed guidelines and regulations. McFarland was primarily responsible for producing the rent-supplement rules, for example. Most public housing guidelines were written by Joseph Burstein, who was responsible for devising the turnkey concept in public housing and implementing it administratively. Robert McCabe played the major role in writing urban renewal guidelines, including the 1967 edict to reorder priorities.

In certain cases, the program administrators may be bypassed in favor of greater control by the Secretary's office. The 1967–68 changes came out of a rather routine internal task force on urban summer problems, which was translated into a policy-making body when the Detroit riot erupted during the weekend of its final meeting. Weaver asked the task force, nominally run by Ralph Taylor, to come up with some ideas for immediate HUD implementation to be presented to the President at the end of the day. The Secretary took four proposals directly to the President and threw his weight behind a number of others which he asked to be staffed out.

One of these was increased citizen participation in the urban renewal program, which Secretary Weaver requested the new Office of Community Development under James Banks, former Director of the District of Columbia's Poverty Program, to draw up. The Office of Community Development wrote a proposal to create Project Area Committees (PAC) consisting of residents of the project areas in all renewal projects. The PAC would have "clear and direct access to decision-making in all stages of the urban renewal process." [7] The urban renewal program people fought this vigorously and emerged with a compromise in which only renewal areas where 20 percent or more of the project consisted of rehabilitation would be required to utilize PAC's. Weaver, however, objected to the compromise formula and, according to one observer, "literally forced the PAC's down the throat of RAA." The final language required citizens committees "for all urban renewal projects which involve residential rehabilitation and which are not yet in execution." [8]

As this example suggests, in cases where an important redistributive change is required for guidelines already in existence, the impetus is likely to come from the Secretary's office. Therefore, normal means of rule-writing are bypassed, since those who administer the programs directly have a vested interest in maintaining the present highly routinized manner of doing so. This explains why the changes in urban renewal relocation, public housing, and FHA guidelines which burst out of HUD during the last half of 1967 and first half of 1968 all emanated from the Secretary's office and involved, in most cases, substantial opposition from the lower-level bureaucracies.

Indeed, in the important decisions, regardless of whether they were new guidelines or changes in existing ones, the Secretary's office was usually involved from the very start. In drawing up the model cities guidelines, for example, Undersecretary Robert Wood was a frequent participant. The process of formulating guidelines involves not only clearance through the General Counsel's and

[7] Department of Housing and Urban Development Local Public Agency Letter No. 458, July 15, 1968, p. 1.
[8] *Ibid.*

Secretary's office (with important decisions being made by the Secretary himself), but also a more informal, but nonetheless real form of clearance with several outside groups. In model cities, drafts of the guidelines were sent around for comments at every stage. A participant observed that the three most important critics in order of importance were: (1) Congress, particularly the House Appropriations Subcommittee; (2) the mayors through their organizations, the United States Conference of Mayors and the National League of Cities; [9] (3) other concerned federal agencies, particularly the Bureau of the Budget. He then added, "several people could have said no to the guidelines and made that 'no' stick: the President, Secretary Weaver, Budget Director Schultze, the head of House Appropriations, or the Conference of Mayors."

Depending on the budget examiners involved, the Bureau of the Budget may play a significant role in devising guidelines and regulations. Any new forms must be cleared by the Budget Bureau before they are issued, and new program operating procedures require new forms. Thus, in some cases the Bureau held up issuance of forms until the examiner was satisfied by the agency. However, as a Budget Bureau respondent concluded:

The examiner's influence here is more in terms of his own interest and of his implied authority. In housing, Budget has had some input on operating procedures, but frankly, 90 percent of the regulations go by the boards, simply because we don't have enough time to follow up on it. There is also some sense of self-restraint on the part of the Budget Bureau. We try to stimulate a sense of responsibility on the part of agencies by questioning them to ensure that they consult and come to agreement with one another. Thus, one of our particular interests was to ensure that FHA and the public housing people set forth regulations consistent with one another.

Because of the possible importance of both the Budget Bureau and the appropriations committees, HUD's own Budget Office, which has intimate contacts with both, is often drawn into the

[9] The organizations vary according to the topic. Thus, in drawing up guidelines for the new open-housing law, organizations such as the Urban League and NAACP were consulted.

guidelines process, particularly if trouble is discerned. In 1965 when the appropriations were refused for rent supplements because of the outcry over the preliminary guidelines, revision of the guidelines was put in the hands of John Frantz, the Budget Officer, Irving Margulies of the General Counsel's Office (which also has close liaison with Congress), and Henry Schechter of the Secretary's office.

Other agencies, such as HEW, OEO, and Labor, also have an interest in HUD's programs. In 1967, the President announced that HUD would chair a committee composed of representatives of agencies engaged in disputes which dealt with urban affairs. The committee has not been notably productive.

## Carrying Out Guidelines

The issuance of edicts does not always mean that they will be carried out immediately and conscientiously. Opposition in the lower bureaucracy may effectively thwart the very intention of the guidelines. Thus, although FHA's top leadership became, according to most respondents, much more concerned with social programs over the course of the 1960's, its regional and local offices which makes day-to-day decisions apparently did not. President Kennedy's Executive Order of November, 1962, banning discrimination in any new homes or apartments financed through government mortgages was never really an effective FHA policy at the operating levels. Thus, the American Friends Service Committee, which did an extensive study of the impact of the Executive Order, concluded in their May, 1967, report:

1. Executive Order 11063 is being widely and flagrantly violated by builders, brokers, and lenders.
2. Implementation of the Order by the Federal Housing Administration (FHA) and the Veterans Administration (VA) has been at best ineffective, and at worst subversive of the goal of equal opportunity in housing.[10]

10 American Friends Service Committee, *A Report to the President on Equal Opportunity in Housing* (Philadelphia: American Friends Service Committee, May, 1967), p. 1.

The report continued:

More disturbing and more harmful than the industry's disregard of the imperatives of the Executive Order have been the inertia, obstruction, and lack of sympathy AFSC has found in the two Federal agencies charged with primary responsibility for enforcing the nondiscrimination and equal opportunity requirements in federally assisted private housing.[11]

FHA responded to this kind of criticism slowly, but it did respond. It issued a series of guidelines revisions in 1967, including one specifically forbidding "redlining" Negro neighborhoods—that is, forbidding loans in entire neighborhoods because they were Negro. Whether these edicts were followed on the everyday operational level, however, is not at all certain, given the close ties of local FHA personnel to the local financial organizations.

## Output and Feedback

The output of the operations subsystem has already been discussed above. Feedback comes into the subsystem from a variety of perspectives. The first and most direct form comes from the lower-level bureaucrats of HUD itself—including those in its regional offices—who must work with the guidelines. Other feedback comes in from the plethora of interests which are affected by HUD programs, from local builders and citizens' groups to national organizations of architects or mayors. Despite the high drama involved in the other three housing policy subsystems, it is indisputable that most of the activity of the housing policy system occurs in this final, though less spectacular, subsystem. The most persistent note in this chorus of feedback concerns the amount of red tape involved in HUD programs. From time to time every Administration issues edicts proclaiming a war on red tape and proclaiming efforts to cut the time required for completing the process (any process) in half. These efforts have not been notably successful.

[11] *Ibid.*, p. 2.

# CHAPTER 8

# The Decision-making Elite

## Institution, Formal Position, and Resource Base

The sixty-seven men and a woman selected as the decision-making elite represented a variety of perspectives within the housing policy process. The distribution was as follows.[1]

| | |
|---|---|
| Congressmen—substantive committees | 12 |
| Congressmen—appropriations committees | 7 |
| Congressional assistants | 7 |
| HUD officials | 14 |
| Executive Office of the President | 8 |
| State and local governments (or groups representing them) | 7 |
| Industry representatives (homebuilders, mortgage bankers, etc.) | 5 |
| "Public interest" representatives (labor, civil rights groups, NAHRO, NHC, etc.) | 7 |
| Other | 1 |

The list encompasses most, but not all, of the highest formal positions within the Executive Office, HUD, and the relevant congressional committees. Included are:

The Special Assistant to the President
Director of the Bureau of the Budget

[1] For a complete list of names of influentials, see Appendix 3.

Assistant Director, Human Resources Program Division, Bureau of the Budget

Assistant Director, Housing and Urban Development, Human Resources Program Division, Bureau of the Budget

Secretary, Department of Housing and Urban Development

Undersecretary, HUD

Deputy Undersecretary, HUD

Assistant Secretary for Mortgage Credit, HUD

Assistant Secretary for Demonstrations and Intergovernmental Relations (Model Cities), HUD

Budget Director, HUD

Chairman, House Banking and Currency Committee

Chairman, House Appropriations Committee

Chairman, House Independent Offices Subcommittee, Appropriations Committee

Chairman, Senate Banking and Currency Committee and Subcommittee on Housing

Chairman, Senate Subcommittee on Urban Affairs, Committee on Appropriations

Not included, however, are:

Assistant Secretary for Housing and Renewal Assistance

General Counsel, HUD

Chairman, House Subcommittee on Housing, Banking and Currency Committee

Chairman, Senate Appropriations Committee

It should be noted here that the previous occupants of the General Counsel's office and the holder of the chairmanship of the House Housing Subcommittee were among the most important of the influentials. HUD's Assistant Secretary for Housing and Renewal Assistance was a new position which merged the HHFA offices of Urban Renewal Commissioner and Public Housing Commissioner (both of which, at times, had powerful occupants). At the time of the study, only one person had held the newly created office.

What this suggests is that formal position is a good resource base for power, providing some other condition is also met by the holders of these positions. In housing, it seemed quite clear that the other condition was some degree of expertise. The required level may not have been high; but housing *is* a complex subject and some understanding above that of the layman is necessary in order to influence policy. Thus, the occupants of all four of the noninfluential formal positions listed above were frequently cited for their lack of expertise. A not atypical comment about one of them was, "He's a very nice person, but he really is nothing but an old pol. He has no idea what's going on." The two HUD positions held by noninfluentials were apparently purposefully filled by non-experts [2] in order to downgrade the excessive influence of former holders of those positions. The Housing subcommittee chairmanship was, of course, filled by the vagaries of the congressional seniority system.

The offices, in short, held in them enough elements of power so that men who had an understanding and feeling for the policy they were dealing with could have an effect on that policy. This is not to imply that all competent holders of similar offices were equally influential, nor that the positions varied directly in influence according to the formal hierarchy of the organization chart. Clearly, with expertise held constant, the relative distribution of other personal and political variables made some holders of a particular office veritable powerhouses, and others nearly powerless. In some instances, underlings wielded significantly more influence than superiors—although generally speaking there did seem to be a relationship between place on the organization chart and degree of influence.

The conclusion that formal position is an important resource base for influence has often been rejected as "naive" or too simple

[2] See Chap. 6.

by political scientists. It is suspect because it does not get underneath formal description to analyze what is really going on. Herbert Simon writes:

There has been some tendency in the literature of political science to regard ordinary sanctions, like money and physical force, as the bases of "effective" power; and legitimacy as the base of "formal" power. The implication of this kind of language is that "effective" power is what determines actual behavior, while "formal" power is some kind of epiphenomenal rationalization of the power structure—window dressing, so to speak.[3]

Yet neither money nor physical force is an important resource base in this instance, whereas formal position indisputably is. Next to formal position, expertise, as has been suggested, is an important base for influence. Most of the influential HUD officials not holding high formal offices had nothing but their claim to expertise to explain their influence. Similarly, representatives of some of the professional organizations (NAHRO, MBA) owed their influence, or at least a good part of it, to their expertise in various aspects of housing policy.

Another important resource base is the ability to mobilize political support. Labor representatives are influential, for example, not simply because they possess expertise, but because labor support and financial contributions are vitally necessary to the election of many Congressmen. The same is also true—though to a somewhat lesser extent than for other groups—of such groups as the homebuilders (NAHB) and the mortgage financing organizations, which have powerful members in almost every Congressional district. In the same vein, individual Congressmen may use their ability to mobilize support as a means of influencing policy. Representative Robert Stephens (D–Ga.), himself a Southern moderate, was influential because he had developed the reputation of being able to carry other Southern moderates along on Administration housing

[3] Herbert Simon, "Notes on the Observation and Measurement of Political Power," *Introductory Readings in Political Behavior*, ed. S. Sidney Ulmer (Chicago: Rand McNally, 1961), p. 370.

bills once they were modified so they were acceptable to him.

Finally, as has been noted under President Johnson, policy was formulated in such a way that a variety of sectors of society were represented in the process of policy formulation.[4] The resource base of individuals chosen for "representative" task forces was therefore likely to be the very societal institution from which the influential came—labor, business, homebuilding, civil rights, etc. Although this factor may account for his having had influence in the first place, an individual's relative influence within the task-force considerations was likely to depend on both his expertise and his ability to articulate and argue his position.

### Role

In any system of human interreactions, there will be a number of roles which describe the behavior of different individuals within that system. In some cases, of course, the same individual may play more than one role, either simultaneously or at different times. A role, once developed, becomes an *expected* pattern of behavior, so that it may be difficult for an influential who is perceived in one role (and may perceive himself thus) to step out of character and retain his influence while playing another role.

Investigation uncovered seven basic roles existing within the housing policy system: decision-maker, delegate, expert, broker, innovator, overseer, and administrator. These roles differed somewhat according to the various subsystem under consideration, but essentially they can be described as follows:

1. Decision-maker—influencing decisions according to an individual's own evaluation of what the needs are.

2. Delegate—influencing decisions according to explicit instructions from an organization or superior.

3. Expert—advising policy-makers on the basis of knowledge possessed in the field of housing.

4. Broker—attempting to bring together divergent views to ar-

[4] See Chap. 5.

rive at a policy which is acceptable to all.

5. Innovator—acting as a generator of new ideas and proposals.

6. Overseer—either providing resources for the carrying out of housing programs or the review of performance of those who are carrying them out.

7. Administrator—carrying out decisions made by others.

Influentials were asked which roles they perceived themselves as playing.[5] Although seven roles seemed identifiable, only six roles emerged. No influential saw himself primarily as an administrator carrying out decisions made by others. As could be expected among a group of highly influential decision-makers, the largest number thought of themselves primarily as decision-makers (See Table 5).

Table 5. Top Role Perceptions of Influentials

| Role perception | First choice of influentials |
|---|---|
| Decision-maker | 16 |
| Delegate | 3 |
| Expert | 12 |
| Broker | 5 |
| Innovator | 5 |
| Overseer | 3 |
| All or some combination equally | 11 |
| Other | 2 |
| No answer | 11 |

The influentials were not only asked to identify the role they most often found themselves playing, but also roles they played with some frequency. Thus, at one time or another, forty decision-makers—nearly 70 percent of those who answered the question— saw themselves as decision-makers.[6] (See Table 6.)

[5] They were given simply descriptions of each role, not the names above.

[6] It is wise to emphasize that the variable being examined here is *self-perceived* roles. It would be much more useful if we could determine what differ-

*Table 6. All Role Perceptions of Influentials*

| Role perception | Number who played role | Percent of those answering |
|---|---|---|
| Decision-maker | 40 | 69% |
| Delegate | 17 | 29 |
| Expert | 24 | 41 |
| Broker | 21 | 36 |
| Innovator | 28 | 48 |
| Overseer | 7 | 12 |

## Socio-economic Background and a Representative Decision-making Elite

Some recent research has dealt with the representativeness of decision-makers by comparing the distribution of a variety of socio-economic variables among decision-makers with the distribution of these same variables among the population. Most of this research, inspired by the realization of political scientists that bureaucrats may be deeply involved in policy as well as administration, has been concerned especially with the problem of a representative bureaucracy. Norton Long sets forth the problem normatively-oriented political scientists have faced with this discovery.

The amoral concept of administrative neutrality is the natural complement of the concept of bureaucracy as instrument; for according to this view the seat of reason and conscience reside in the legislature . . . and a major, if not the major, task for constitutionalism is the maintenance of the supremacy of the legislature over the bureaucracy.

[However] the most ardent advocate of legislative supremacy can no longer blink at the fact of administrative discretion and even administrative legislation. . . . The bureaucracy is in policy, and major policy, to

ence, if any, these self-perceptions made on actual behavior. Thus, do those who see themselves as decision-makers act differently than those who view themselves as experts? Unfortunately this is impossible to determine with this data.

stay. . . . Growth in the power of the bureaucracy is looked upon as a menace to constitutionalism. By some it is seen as a dangerous enhancement of the power of the President, by others as an alarming accretion of power to a non-elective part of the government. The logic of either-or sees a cumulative process in which the supremacy of the elected legislature is replaced by the supremacy of an appointed bureaucracy.[7]

Long, however, feels the problem is a false one, for the bureaucracy, he claims, actually is representative.

Accustomed as we are to the identification of election with both representation and democracy, it seems strange at first to consider that the non-elected civil service may be both more representative of the country and more democratic in its composition than the Congress. As it operates in the civil service, the recruitment process brings into Federal employment and positions of national power, persons whose previous affiliation, training, and background cause them to conceive of themselves as representing constituencies that are relatively uninfluential in Congress. . . .

The bureaucracy now has a very real claim to be considered much more representative of the American people in its composition than the Congress. This is not merely the case with respect to the class structure of the country but, equally significant with respect to the learned groups, skills, economic interests, races, nationalities, and religions. The rich diversity that makes up the United States is better represented in its civil service than anywhere else.[8]

Several recent books have provided tests for Long's theory.[9] All have had difficulties selecting which bureaucrats specifically to study. Long himself, for example, claims that the civil service as a whole is democratic and representative, yet it is clear that most policy initiatives reside high up in the bureaucracy and are concentrated in the hands of political executives who are not appointed through traditional civil service procedures at all. Warner studied 13,000 high civil servants and political appointees; Stanley,

[7] Norton Long, "Bureaucracy and Constitutionalism," *The Politics of the Federal Bureaucracy*, ed. Alan Altshuler (New York: Dodd, Mead & Co., 1968), pp. 17–19.

[8] *Ibid.*, pp. 21–22.

[9] See W. Lloyd Warner, Paul P. Van Riper, Norman H. Martin, and Orvis F. Collins, *The American Federal Executive* (New Haven, Conn.: Yale Uni-

Mann, and Doig studied the political executives; while Mann and Doig studied the second-level political executives. None selected their sample on the basis of who actually made policy decisions in the bureaucracy unless they assumed that influence was coterminous with high formal position. Stanley, Mann, and Doig—who studied the highest political executives—seemingly contradict Long's hypotheses. They conclude:

Federal political executives are not representative of the general population, or even of the educated, financially stable population. They are representative of persons who have an affinity for public service and demonstrated ability to run large enterprises or to give specialized aid to those who run them. . . . These executives were hired to run the government and the recruitment process, generally speaking, has been an effort to get the best people for that purpose, even if their unrepresentativeness of the general population may result in occasional strains.[10]

Donald Matthews has extended this kind of analysis to political decision-makers in general, although he too chooses solely by formal position. Reviewing data from Presidents and Vice Presidents, U.S. Senators and Representatives, Cabinet members, high-level civil servants, state governors, and state legislators, he concludes that "our political decision-makers, taken as a whole, are very far from being a cross section of the electorate. Rather, there seems to be a sort of class ranking of public offices in the United States— the more important the office, the higher the social status of its normal incumbent."[11]

The present study has encompassed those decision-makers deemed to be most powerful within a particular policy system. Although there seems to be no compelling reason to consider socioeconomic variables as a particularly good index of representa-

versity Press, 1963); also David T. Stanley, Dean E. Mann, and Jameson W. Doig, *Men Who Govern* (Washington, D.C.: The Brookings Institution, 1967) and Dean E. Mann and Jameson W. Doig, *The Assistant Secretaries* (Washington, D.C.: The Brookings Institution, 1965).

[10] Stanley, Mann, and Doig, *ibid.*, pp. 79–80.

[11] Donald Matthews, *The Social Background of Political Decisionmakers* (New York: Random House, 1954), p. 32.

tion,[12] it may be interesting to describe the decision-makers in this light, simply to add a comparative element to previous studies which have utilized this framework.

An analysis of the social background of the sixty-eight housing decision-makers reveals some interesting, if hardly startling facts. The housing decision-makers grew up largely in urban areas. (See Table 7.)

**Table 7. Classification of Decision-Makers, by Place Raised**

| Where raised | Percent of total |
| --- | --- |
| City | 57% |
| Suburb | 7 |
| Small town | 28 |
| Farm | 6 |
| Not able to determine | 1 |

A clear majority of the decision-makers were raised in city environments at a time in which only about one-third of the population resided in cities. Since the median age of the decision-makers is between forty-six and fifty years of age, the 1930 census provides the best indication of what the United States was like during their formative years. In 1930, 34.9 percent of the population resided in urban areas of 50,000 or more. Whether the overrepresentation of city-dwellers in the decision-making elite is due to a relative lack of interest non-city-dwellers might have in housing—which is widely perceived as an urban problem—or whether it is due to intervening variables associated with city life, is impossible to determine from the data.

The decision-makers also were mostly Easterners; only 23 percent

---

[12] Except as socio-economic variables might also account for attitudes of decision-makers. But that in itself is in need of empirical investigation. At any rate, if attitudes are what one is interested in, then it is surely better to study attitudes directly. See p. 173 ff. in the present text.

Table 8. *Classification of Decision-Makers, by Section of Country Raised*

| Section of country | Percent of decision- makers | Percent of population 1930[a] | Percent of population 1960[a] |
|---|---|---|---|
| New England | 19% | 6.6% | 5.9% |
| Middle Atlantic | 16 | 21.3 | 19.1 |
| East North Central | 24 | 20.5 | 20.2 |
| West North Central | 10 | 10.8 | 8.6 |
| South Atlantic | 9 | 12.8 | 14.5 |
| East South Central | 6 | 8.0 | 6.7 |
| West South Central | 7 | 9.9 | 9.5 |
| Mountain & Pacific | 6 | 10.0 | 15.6 |
| No answer | 3 | — | — |

[a] United States Department of Commerce, Bureau of the Census, *United States Census of Population 1960, United States Summary, Number of Inhabitants* (Washington, D.C.: United States Government Printing Office, 1961), pp. 1–19.

of them grew up in states west of the Mississippi River. (See Table 8.)

Thus, the Western segment of the country—and, particularly, the Mountain and Pacific states whose boundaries contain several large cities with major housing problems (Los Angeles, San Francisco, Oakland, Denver, Seattle, etc.)—was substantially underrepresented both in terms of the 1930 and 1960 population. New England, on the other hand, whose cities, because of their physical construction, have housing problems somewhat distinctive from those of other regions, was overrepresented by a factor of more than three. All of this tends to reinforce the findings of Stanley, Mann, and Doig, who concluded that federal political executives were preponderantly "big city boys from the East." [13]

The sex, racial, and ethnic characteristics of housing decision-makers are also quite unrepresentative of the American population. There is only one woman (Representative Sullivan) among the de-

[13] Stanley, Mann, and Doig, *op. cit.* (n. 9), p. 14.

cision-makers, undoubtedly reflecting somewhat more intensively than would be expected the social norms of American life. There are also only two Negroes among the sixty-eight decision-makers, despite the fact that most recent efforts in the policy area have been directed at improving housing for Negroes. On the other hand, nearly 20 percent of the decision-makers are Jewish, despite the fact that only 3 percent of the American population is. This larger representation probably reflects both the easy access of Jews to the bureaucracy relative to other occupations (during the 1930's the federal government made the same kinds of efforts to recruit Jews as it is now doing with blacks) and the traditional Jewish involvement in social welfare concerns.

The characteristic, however, which most distinguishes housing decision-makers from the rest of the American population is education. (See Table 9.)

In 1966, approximately 10 percent of the American people twenty-five years of age and over had completed four years of college or more, while 92 percent of the housing decision-makers had done so.[14] Matthews' data suggests that political decision-makers in gen-

Table 9. Decision-Makers Classified,
   by Level of Education

| Educational level | Percent of decision-makers |
|---|---|
| High school or less | 1% |
| Attended college | 6 |
| College degree | 9 |
| Attended graduate school | 9 |
| Graduate intermediate degree (M.A., M.P.A., etc.) | 15 |
| Doctoral degree | 15 |
| Law degree | 44 |
| No answer | 1 . |

[14] U.S. Bureau of the Census, *Statistical Abstract of the United States: 1967*, 88th Edition (Washington, D.C., 1967), p. 116.

eral are more highly educated than the public. He reports: "There is a good deal of variation in educational level within the group, but it is true that the vast majority of them have been selected in recent years from the 10 percent or so of the adult population who have attended college." [15] The fact that this is so disturbs Matthews. "But while the American educational system is one of the most equalitarian in the world substantial differences in educational opportunity do exist between social classes. . . . Therefore without alterations in the present American educational system, the higher the informal educational requirements are set for political decisionmakers, the more unequal become the political life chances of Americans." [16]

Economics and law were the subjects most frequently pursued by decision-makers. Nearly 50 percent of those who had some graduate work did so in law, while slightly over 20 percent had graduate training in economics. Economics was the leading undergraduate major (30 percent of those whose college major was ascertainable), while history (24 percent) and political science (20 percent) followed. Close knowledge of both economics and law are subjects which, while not absolutely mandatory, are extremely useful for those who work with housing policy. Those who have training in these areas are therefore much more likely to dominate in the housing area.

To emphasize further the nonrepresentative character of the decision-making elite, 82 percent of the sixty-eight decision-makers considered themselves Democrats while an additional 4 percent considered themselves independent-leaning Democrats. This statistic clearly reflects the fact that the study was conducted entirely during the period of a Democratic administration. Stanley, Mann, and Doig show that over 80 percent of political appointments to the federal executive branch made during Democratic administrations since Roosevelt have been Democratic; 76 percent of Eisen-

---

[15] Matthews, *op. cit.* (n. 11), p. 78.
[16] *Ibid.*

hower's appointments, however, were Republican.[17] Although Presidential appointments do not account for all of the non-Congressional decision-makers, they do account for many of them. This obviously brings forth the question of whether the housing decision-making elite would have been significantly different in other salient characteristics had the study been conducted during the time in which a Republican administration was in office. Since there were only seven of sixty-eight respondents who called themselves Republican (and five of those were associated with Congress), the data do not allow for any reliable projections.

The data do show rather conclusively, however, that, at least in socioeconomic and demographic terms, housing decision-makers are not very representative of the American population. As a class they are more urban, more Eastern, more white, much better educated, and much more Democratic than the rest of the population. Some of this is undoubtedly due to self-selection, but it also suggests that the housing decision-making elite may not be easily open to certain strata of the population and that social mobility in America is somewhat less than perfect, particularly for nonwhite groups and groups which do not have any easy access to educational opportunities.

## Decision-makers' Attitudes and Values

As Agger, Goldrich, and Swanson have suggested,[18] a political system cannot be adequately described without reference to the attitudes of its decision-makers on substantive questions of policy. Therefore, influentials were asked to respond to a variety of questions concerning their attitudes towards housing-related questions as well as their views on the need for social change and the speed with which it should come. For purposes of comparison, answers to

[17] Stanley, Mann, and Doig, *op. cit.* (n. 9), p. 24.
[18] Robert Agger, Daniel Goldrich, and Burt Swanson, *The Rulers and the Ruled* (New York: John Wiley, 1964), Chap. 1.

the same questions were obtained from official spokesmen of various organizations concerned in one way or another with housing policy.[19] The spokesmen were speaking directly for their respective organizations.

Influentials were asked two open-ended questions concerning priorities. The first asked what ought to be the top priority in federal government policy towards urban areas. In virtually every case, the top priority was directed towards aiding low-income people in one way or another. Similar answers prevailed to the second question, which asked what ought to be the top priorities in federal government housing policy. The answers to both of these questions undoubtedly reflect the very recent emphasis on poverty and race as major problem areas in American life. It is exceedingly doubtful that, even ten years ago, nearly as many answers would have focused on poverty. Rather, it is suspected, more answers would have emphasized problems of urban sprawl, the decline of the central business district, or the need for more professional planning.

Influentials were also asked to name a top priority in a functional area. Interestingly, housing ranked well behind employment as a priority among housing influentials. (See Table 10.)

The groups concerned with housing policy in their answers split

Table 10. Top Priority in Functional Area,
by Influentials and Groups

| Top priority | Influentials | Groups |
|---|---|---|
| Employment | 21 | 5 |
| Not able to select between functional areas (too interrelated) | 16 | 2 |
| Housing | 15 | 4 |
| Welfare | 2 | 1 |
| Education | 2 | |
| Other or no answer | 12 | 5 |

[19] See Chap. 4.

in approximately the same manner as the influentials did. However, there were two groups pressing priorities which were advocated by nobody within the decision-making elite. SNCC felt top priority ought to go to a huge influx of federal money directly to black communities with no string attached. If there might be difficulty in determining to whom in black communities the money ought to be given, SNCC would solve this problem easily enough: "We would tell them." Another group, the American Institute of Planners, felt that top priority should be given to reorganizing federal government structures so that planning would play a more prominent role in policy formulation.

The influentials were asked to suggest the changes in direction they would like to see policy take. Answers to this open-ended question varied greatly, but several distinct categories emerged clearly from the analysis. (Each influential was assigned to only one category, on the basis of the change in direction he mentioned first, despite the fact that he might have mentioned several changes of directions.) The most frequent answer was that more funding for present programs—and thus greater volume—was needed. Second most frequently cited was the need for more incentives to involve private enterprise. (See Table 11).

Several of the groups answered in terms of policy directions that

Table 11. Direction of Housing Policy Desired, by Influentials and Groups

| Direction of housing policy desired | Influentials | Groups |
|---|---|---|
| (a) More funding and production | 16 | 6 |
| (b) Incentives to involve private industry | 12 | 2 |
| (c) Subsidy to consumer | 11 | 2 |
| (d) Attacking environmental constraints (codes, lands, etc.) inhibiting supply | 8 | 1 |
| (e) Improvement of administration of management | 7 | 0 |
| (f) Community building | 3 | 0 |
| (g) Other and no answer | 10 | 6 |

were not represented within the decision-making elite. Three of the four nonrepresented answers were from Negro or civil rights groups. SNCC again suggested that government programs were irrelevant since "white folk aren't going to do anything for black folk anyway"; they advocated money payments directly to the black community. CORE argued that the greatest need was to understand the psychology of black people and that the way to accomplish this was to allow blacks to speak for themselves and express their own needs. The NAACP called for a rejection of the approach of local initiative and its plan to "permit the Federal Government to directly acquire, clean up, and rebuild slum areas." The AIP felt a need for more federal research into housing.

Finally, the respondent influentials were asked a series of shorter questions about various issues of housing policy. The first asked whether it was "proper for the Federal Government to intervene in the housing market in order to aid low-income families obtain housing." It was largely in terms of the proper role of the federal government in American society that the debate over housing policies during the 1930's was carried on. Yet, the answers to this series of shorter questions give credence to those who have argued that the New Deal has been accepted and the issues are now differently defined. All sixty-three respondents who answered the question felt that such intervention into the private economy *was* a proper function of the federal government. The groups were also unanimous in their approval.

Another question about federal role evoked somewhat more disagreement, but not nearly as much, it is suspected, as it would have even five or ten years ago. The respondents were asked whether it was proper for the federal government "to devise policies to achieve social and racial integration at the neighborhood level." Fifty of the decision-makers replied that it was proper, while twelve objected that it was not. Of the twelve opposed, eight were Congressmen (eight Congressmen were also in favor), a fact which undoubtedly reflects the intensity of this issue in the mass public as well as an overrepresentation of Southerners among the Congressional decision-makers. The groups divided in about the same proportion. Ten said they thought such action was within the proper sphere of governmental activity, two opposed it outright, and three groups replied that opinion in their organization would be divided on the question and that the organization had taken no position on it. The five groups in the last two categories were all housing-industry organizations.

While there appeared to be little disagreement that it was proper for the federal government to involve itself in an effort to solve social problems, there *was* great disagreement over the exact direction programs to solve these problems should take and over who should control those programs. Thus, influentials were asked whether "public policy should be directed more towards: (a) improving housing conditions within the ghetto; (b) dispersing the ghetto; or (c) both in about equal proportions." The answer to this question several years ago would have been a good test for separating racial liberals from racial conservatives, the liberals favoring dispersal while the conservatives opting for the "segregating" response of maintaining the ghetto albeit in an improved condition. The Negro Revolution, however, has changed all this. (See Table 12).

The thirty-one who favored "both in about equal proportions" probably reflected the basic ambivalence which afflicts many "liberals" on this question. Indeed, the nineteen advocating improving the ghetto represented a curious coalition of racial conservatives and social activists. Included in the nineteen were six of the twelve

Table 12. Public Policy Towards Ghettos,
        by Influentials and Groups

| Public policy | Influentials | Groups |
|---|---|---|
| Improving the ghetto | 19 | 2 |
| Dispersing | 8 | 2 |
| Both in about equal proportions | 31 | 8 |
| Other | 3 | 0 |
| No answer | 7 | 5 |

who had opposed federal action to achieve integration. Alongside of these were many who agreed with groups such as CORE that the major effort had to go into improving life in the ghetto, which is where most poor Negroes (they argued) realistically will be for years to come.

A question dealing with what kinds of programs would most effectively end the slums uncovered more disagreement. The influentials were asked to designate which alternatives they favored and to rank them in order of importance. Impressive support was shown for a guaranteed employment and minimum income program, which received nearly twice as many first-place rankings as any of the other three approaches. However, at the same time, significant opposition was apparent since eighteen respondents of the sixty-one who answered refused to rank such a program at all. (See Table 13.)

Table 13. Best Way of Ending Ghettos, by Influentials and Groups

| Program | Influentials | | Groups | |
|---|---|---|---|---|
| | First place rank | No rank | First place rank | No rank |
| Guaranteed employment and income | 27 | 18 | 6 | 2 |
| Standard housing for all | 14 | 10 | 3 | |
| Improved government social services | 7 | 16 | 0 | 2 |
| Mobilize slum residents for political action | 3 | 26 | 1 | 2 |
| Other (all equally or more than one unranked) | 10 | | 2 | |
| No answer | 7 | | 5 | |

Eleven of the eighteen opposed to guaranteed employment and income were Congressmen, suggesting that such a program, despite the obvious momentum it has generated within a relatively short time, would still have hard sailing when it comes before Congress. That it had gained momentum was suggested by the fact that four of the eight White House officials ranked guaranteed employment first (only one was unalterably opposed).

In some ways it appears that the New Deal debate over the role of the federal government has evolved into a dispute over control. The influentials were split fairly evenly in their responses to the question: "Should low-income housing policy be devised to give more control over policy decisions than is presently the case to (a) the Federal Government or (b) local governments?" (See Table 14.)

Table 14. Control of Programs,
    by Influentials and Groups

| More control to | Influentials | Groups |
|---|---|---|
| Federal | 23 | 7 |
| Local | 28 | 6 |
| About right now | 5 | 0 |
| No answer | 12 | 4 |

The lineup of forces again proved interesting. Eleven of fifteen of the Congressmen who answered joined five of the six local officials who answered in favoring more control at the local level, despite the fact that many of the Congressmen involved would be considered "conservative," while most of the local officials would be considered "liberal." On the other hand five of the six White House officials answering found themselves on the same side as all four representatives of housing-industry organizations answering in favor of a stronger federal role. The housing industry, despite a reputation for conservatism, has long complained that they are at the mercy of arbitrary, archaic, and costly local building codes and zoning laws.

With the advent of the poverty program another question of control was brought to the level of public debate. The influentials were asked: "On decisions concerning low-income housing which must be made at the local level, should control reside (a) in the duly elected public officials and established public agencies, or (b)

in community residents who are most affected by the decisions?"
An overwhelming number of influentials replied that control must
rest with the public officials, but a large number also volunteered
that this must go hand in hand with a good deal of consultation of
and participation by community residents. (See Table 15.)

Table 15. Who Should Control,
by Influentials and Groups

| Who should control | Influentials | Groups |
|---|---|---|
| Duly elected public offi-<br>cials | 30 | 7 |
| Public officials (but some<br>form of community par-<br>ticipation volunteered) | 21 | 3 |
| Community residents | 7 | 5 |
| No answer | 10 | 2 |

For the first time there seems to be a markedly different distribution of opinion among groups than among decision-makers. Three
of the four black or civil rights organizations—SNCC, CORE, and
the NAACP—favored control by community residents, as did another group which has attempted to forge working relationships
with the black community, the Urban Coalition. These groups
have concentrated much of their attack against established institutions and programs on the basis of the lack of citizen participation
in community decisions. It would appear that the attack has had
some effect, although perhaps not enough to satisfy the groups
making the demands. Nine of the fourteen HUD officials volunteered that some form of community participation was necessary
(one favored community control), undoubtedly reflecting rather
new concern in the Department born of the constant attacks they
had undergone from 1964 to this writing.[20] Five of the six local officials answering the question predictably favored control by themselves.

[20] See Chap. 7.

## What Does It Mean?

As was suggested in Chapter 1, political scientists ought to be particularly interested in the degree of convergence (or divergence) of decision-makers' attitudes on questions involving policy. Convergence, however, is a relative concept; its degree can only be determined by comparison with the range of attitudes held by those who are outside the policy system. If the range of attitudes within the system is significantly less wide than the range outside the system, then the system is convergent. If the range of attitudes within the system approaches that outside the system, then the system is divergent.[21] In the housing policy system it appeared that, at least on questions dealing with the direction of policy, elite opinion was relatively divergent with respect to the organized groups.

If, however, attitudes are compared not with outside groups, but with logically possible alternatives, a different picture emerges.

Thus, no decision-maker and only one group (the NAACP) suggested moving in the direction of a "federal approach" to housing, certainly a logically possible alternative. Indeed, the national government approach is the normal way of doing business for many European countries.[22] However, within the decision-making elite

[21] Ideally, one would like to be able to use attitudes within the general population to compare to attitudes of decision-makers within the housing policy system. However, no such data were available and obtaining them would have been far beyond the scope of the study. Instead, attitudes of spokesmen of groups concerned with housing policy were used for the comparison. (See Chap. 4 for a description of these groups and how they were selected.) It might be objected, of course, that the use of organized groups is inadequate since significant bodies of opinion within the mass public may not be translated into organized group representation. (See Chapter I.) However, the groups were selected carefully in order to include all ranges of opinion that were organized. Furthermore, since SNCC and CORE were included (even though these groups do not play a major role in decision-making), the large body of opinion most often pointed to as unrepresented—that of the Negro poor—is included here.

[22] D. V. Donnison, The Government of Housing (Baltimore: Penguin Books, 1967), Chap. 3.

in this country there seems to be an unstated consensus that, whatever changes might be made, they will be within the framework of local initiative, local site selection, and building by private concerns. Since only one outside group volunteered this alternative, it seems fair to conclude that its lack of consideration is probably due more to cultural predisposition than to any real lack of representativeness of the decision-making elite.

The above analysis would seem to suggest that the housing policy elite is representative (divergent), but only within a fairly strict framework defining what is permissible policy in the United States. Thus the possibility that the federal government might take the initiative, select sites, and build housing itself is simply outside the realm of discussion in the United States at the present time. Outside the realm also is any arrangement which would provide visible government subsidies to those who are capable of purchasing suitable housing on the private market.

# CHAPTER 9

# Conclusion

Modern political science has, for the most part, shied away from the study of public policy. This is no doubt due to the prescriptive and normative approach which characterized earlier policy studies and which fell into great disfavor with the advent of objective and empirical political science. Policy studies survived primarily in the form of case studies, justified more in terms of useful teaching devices than in terms of adding to the sum of research on the American political system. That this is not a healthy situation has apparently been recognized by a growing number of political scientists who feel that policy—the output of the political system—is surely worthy of study by political scientists.[1]

There also appears to be no inherent reason why policy should not be readily susceptible to study by empirical scientists. Political science has developed, over the past two decades, a rich variety of conceptual frameworks which have served to order and organize political research. The concept of the political system has proven particularly rewarding for this purpose. Surely there is no reason why a policy area cannot be viewed in this light. Political scientists would then engage in the study of political behavior within a political system defined analytically by the interaction of individu-

---

[1] See, for example, Raymond A. Bauer and Kenneth J. Gergen, eds., *The Study of Policy Formulation* (Toronto: The Free Press, 1968); also Austin Ranney, ed., *Political Science and Public Policy* (Chicago: Markham Publishing Co., 1968).

als involved in the making of policy decisions in a particular policy area.[2]

The present study of the housing political system has thus been an attempt to describe and analyze a policy area in the above terms. It is not claimed that this is the *only* way to study public policy, but rather that it is a particularly useful way for a political scientist to do so, one firmly grounded in the framework of recent political research. Indeed, such an approach closely parallels some of the work which has been done in the area of power studies of community political systems, since the first step in analyzing the policy system was to identify the main actors whose interaction defined that system.

Despite the enormous contributions the power studies have made, however, they have recently come under some searching criticism.[3] Preoccupation with terming an entire community political system "pluralist" or "elitist" by students of community power has, according to critics, ignored variations in types of political decisions which a political system handles. Political scientists have generally concentrated on distributive rather than redistributive types of political decisions; thus their conclusions about the nature of the political system may very well be biased. Because redistributive decisions are likely, at any rate, to be more important for the political system than distributive ones, this study has concentrated on redistributive decisions in the housing political system. The focus on redistributive decisions yielded interesting results particularly in the area of appropriations, where some standard conclusions about the Congressional appropriations process were found to be of dubious value when redistributive rather than distributive decisions were under scrutiny.

Many of the community power studies were also found lacking in their conception of the policy process since they did not distinguish between different stages. In this study, four relatively distinct stages of the policy process were identified at the federal

[2] Or areas, since this easily lends itself to a comparative approach.
[3] See p. 7.

level (the number and character of the stages might well differ at the level of communities). These could be considered subsystems of the more general policy system under consideration. These stages were: (1) policy formulation, (2) substantive legislation, (3) appropriations, and (4) operations. Each of these stages was necessary to successfully carry out a positive policy decision; each of them could, in effect, exercise a veto power over taking a particular positive action.

The most striking fact about the housing political system was the degree to which the system's environment constrained the range of decisions open to the system. The broader economic and political situation, in particular the Vietnam War and consequent high interest rates throughout the economy, not only largely defined the nature of the problem to be dealt with, but also largely prescribed the manner with which it would be dealt.

Input from organized interest groups—which often formed the basis of traditional case studies of public policy—was found to be relatively unimportant in influencing major redistributive housing decisions, although quite important in more incremental distributive decisions. Particularly in the subsystem of policy formulation, organized interest groups seemed to lack major impact; instead White House task forces provided the main input in this subsystem. Sectors of society rather than specific organized interests were represented within these task forces.

In the conversion process itself, the subsystems were found to be somewhat autonomous. There was some overlapping of membership among members of the various subsystems but it was not extensive.[4] The appropriations subsystem, in particular, was found to be quite autonomous. Different institutions dominated different subsystems. The institutionalized President played the major role in the process of policy formulation, while Congress appeared to be the locus of redistributive decision-making in the substantive legislative and appropriations subsystems of housing. The Depart-

---

[4] See Appendix 2.

ment itself dominated the least visible but not unimportant subsystem, that of operations.

A persistent finding throughout the study concerning the conversion process was that specific individuals could and did make a significant contribution to the nature of policy through force of their own personality or through the chance occurrence of finding themselves in the right place at the right time. As has been noted, broad social, economic, and political forces set the limits on what was or was not possible, but the exact shape of policy (and, in some cases, whether or not there was any positive policy output at all) was determined by individual participants and depended greatly on the nature of these individuals.

The individuals who comprised the housing decision-making elite appeared to utilize formal position and expertise, particularly in law and economics, as their most important resource bases. These resource bases are not widely distributed among the general public and the influentials were therefore hardly representative of the American population in any socioeconomic sense. They were overwhelmingly white, male, and Democratic; they were also disproportionately from urban areas and from the East. In addition, they were highly educated when compared to the general public. Yet, despite this, their attitudes varied widely and the range of attitudes seemed to approach the range of attitudes held by organized groups concerned with housing policy.

The attitudes held by the elite included a consensus that poverty and the problems of low-income citizens were the major problems facing urban areas and that housing low-income people was the major priority so far as housing policy was concerned. Traditional disputes emanating from the New Deal concerning the propriety of the federal government intervening in the housing market appeared to have disappeared; the new disagreement centered upon *what kind* of government policy would be appropriate and who should administer it. In general terms, members of the institutionalized Presidency in particular, and HUD to a lesser extent, proposed major changes such as guaranteed employment and income programs, while Congressmen remained significantly more cautious in proposing changes.

In sum, it appears that the housing political system belongs in the box occupied by pluralist democracy in the typology presented in Chapter 1 (p. 11). Data compiled in Chapter 3 suggest that the housing decision-making elite, although by no means completely closed, is certainly not equally open to groups of widely varying viewpoints. Data in Chapter 8 support the conclusion that the ideology of the leadership, although not perfectly divergent, is fairly representative of the range of opinion in outside groups concerned with housing policy. In short, a relatively small number of groups have effective access to the decision-making elite, but those in the elite themselves hold a range of attitudes which approximates fairly well those views held outside the elite.

This finding coincides generally with the way in which most political scientists have traditionally described the American political system. What many elite critics (C. Wright Mills in particular) of the American political system have often missed is the manner in which the divergent ideologies are differentially distributed at different stages and within different institutions in the decision process. Thus the American political system is one in which power is dispersed throughout various institutions and groups, with no one of them in most cases able to independently exert its will without at least the acquiescence of some others. In housing, for example, it appears that several institutions held what in effect was a veto power over public policy. In most cases, neither the institutional Presidency, Congress, nor HUD could unilaterally declare what form policy would take, but each (and particularly the first two) could determine what it would not be. Thus, those such as C. Wright Mills who ignore Congress' importance by consigning it to the middle levels of power [5] miss a vital point. In redistribution decisions concerning very major and important (not simply middle-level) issues Congress can—and often does—effectively exer-

[5] C. Wright Mills, *The Power Elite* (New York: Oxford University Press, 1957), p. 244.

cise a veto power.

Thus, although the ideology of the entire decision-making elite may indeed be divergent, the ideology of important and relatively autonomous groups within it may be convergent. This seems to be the case with the Congressional decision-makers, as the data in Chapter 8 demonstrate. And since Congressional decision-makers dominate two of the four stages in the housing policy process, their relatively conservative position—particularly of those in the appropriations stage—on certain issues of housing policy becomes a relevant factor in explaining why housing output has apparently lagged behind the more "liberal" outlook of the entire housing decision-making elite.

# Bibliography

Abrams, Charles. *The City is the Frontier*. New York: Harper and Row, 1965.

——. *The Future of Housing*. New York: Harper and Row, 1946.

Agger, Robert G., Daniel Goldrich, and Burt Swanson. *The Rulers and the Ruled*. New York: John Wiley, 1964.

American Friends Service Committee. *A Report to the President on Equal Opportunity in Housing*. Philadelphia: American Friends Service Committee, May, 1967.

Anton, Thomas. "Power, Pluralism, and Local Politics," *Administrative Science Quarterly*, VII (March, 1963), 425–458.

Bachrach, Peter and Morton S. Baratz. "Decisions and non-Decisions: An Analytical Framework," *American Political Science Review*, LVII (September, 1963), 632–642.

Bailey, Stephen. *Congress Makes a Law*. New York: Columbia University Press, 1950.

Bauer, Raymond R. and Kenneth J. Gergen, eds. *The Study of Public Policy Formulation*. Toronto: The Free Press, 1968.

Bellush, Jewel and Murray Hausknecht, eds. *Urban Renewal: People, Politics and Planning*. New York: Anchor Books, 1967.

Bentley, Arthur R. *The Process of Government*. Bloomington, Ind.: Principia Press, 1908.

Beyer, Glenn. *Housing and Society*. New York: MacMillan, 1966.

Burns, James MacGregor. *Presidential Government*. Boston: Houghton Mifflin, 1966.

"Civil Rights Lobbying." *Congressional Quarterly*, April 26, 1968, pp. 931–934.

Connolly, William E. *Political Science and Ideology*. New York: Atherton Press, 1967.

Dahl, Robert A. "A Critique of the Ruling Elite Model," *American Political Science Review*, LII (June, 1958), 463–469.

——. *Modern Political Analysis*. Englewood Cliffs, N.J.: Prentice-Hall, 1963.

——. *Pluralist Democracy in the United States*. Chicago: Rand McNally, 1967.

————. *A Preface to Democratic Theory.* Chicago: University of Chicago Press, 1956.

————. *Who Governs.* New Haven, Conn.: Yale University Press, 1961.

Donnison, D. V. *The Government of Housing.* Baltimore: Penguin Books, 1967.

Drew, Elizabeth. "On Giving Oneself a Hotfoot: Government by Commission," *Atlantic Monthly,* CCXXI (May, 1968), 45–48.

"Drive Begins to Save Rent Supplement 'City Funds'," *Congressional Quarterly,* July 28, 1967, pp. 1317–1319.

Easton, David. *A Framework for Political Analysis.* Englewood Cliffs, N.J.: Prentice-Hall, 1965.

————. *The Political System.* New York: Alfred A. Knopf, 1953.

Ellickson, Robert. "Government Housing Assistance to the Poor," *Yale Law Review,* LXXVI, No. 3 (January, 1967), 508–542.

Fenno, Richard. *The Power of the Purse.* Boston: Little Brown, 1966.

Glazer, Nathan. "Housing Problems and Housing Policies," *The Public Interest,* VII (Spring, 1967), pp. 21–51.

Goodwin, George. Subcommittees: The Miniature Legislatives of Congress," *American Political Science Review,* LXI (Sept., 1962), 596–604.

Greer, Scott. *Urban Renewal and American Cities.* New York: Bobbs-Merrill, 1965.

Grigsby, William. *Housing Markets and Public Policy.* Philadelphia: University of Pennsylvania Press, 1963.

"Home Ownership Bills not Enacted in 1967," *Congressional Quarterly Almanac,* 1967, pp. 492–503.

*Housing a Nation.* Washington, D.C.: *Congressional Quarterly,* 1966.

Hunter, Floyd. *Community Power Structure.* Chapel Hill: University of North Carolina Press, 1953.

Kariel, Henry. *The Decline of American Pluralism.* Stanford: Stanford University Press, 1961.

Katz, Daniel and Robert Kahn. *The Social Psychology of Organizations.* New York: John Wiley, 1966.

Kaufmann, Herbert. *Politics and Policies in State and Local Governments.* Englewood Cliffs, N.J.: Prentice-Hall, 1963.

Lane, Robert. *Political Life.* New York: The Free Press, 1959.

Lasswell, Harold and Abraham Kaplan. *Power and Society.* New Haven: Yale University Press, 1950.

"Lobby Campaign Saves Model Cities Funds in House," *Congressional Quarterly,* June 9, 1967, pp. 979–984.

Long, Norton. "Bureaucracy and Constitutionalism," *The Politics of the*

*Federal Bureaucracy,* ed. Alan Altshuler, pp. 17–26. New York: Dodd, Mead, 1968.

Lowi, Theodore. "Distribution, Regulation, Redistribution: The Function of Government," *Public Policies and Their Functions,* ed. Randall B. Ripley, pp. 27–40. New York: W. W. Norton, 1966.

———. "The Public Philosophy: Interest Group Liberalism," *American Political Science Review,* LXI (March, 1967), 5–24.

McConnell, Grant. *Private Power and American Democracy.* New York: Alfred A. Knopf, 1967.

Maisel, Sherman. *Financing Real Estate.* New York: McGraw-Hill, 1965.

"Major Housing Legislation Enacted," *Congressional Quarterly Almanac,* 1965, pp. 358–381.

Mann, Dean E. and Jameson W. Doig. *The Assistant Secretaries.* Washington, D.C.: The Brookings Institution, 1965.

Marx, Gary T. *Protest and Prejudice: A Study of Belief in the Black Community.* New York: Harper and Row, 1967.

Masters, Nicholas A. "Committee Assignments," *New Perspectives on the House of Representatives,* eds., Robert Peabody and Nelson Polsby, pp. 227–252. 2nd edition. Chicago: Rand McNally, 1969.

Matthews, Donald. *The Social Background of Political Decision-makers.* New York: Random House, 1954.

Meyerson, Martin, Barbara Terrett, and William L.C. Wheaton. *Housing, People, and Cities.* New York: McGraw-Hill, 1962.

Mills, C. Wright. *The Power Elite.* New York: Oxford University Press, 1957.

———. "The Structure of Power in Modern Society," *Power Politics and People,* ed. Irving Lewis Horowitz, pp. 23–38. New York: Ballantine Books, 1963.

Mitchell, William. *The American Polity.* Glencoe, Ill.: The Free Press, 1962.

National Committee Against Discrimination in Housing. *How the Federal Government Builds Ghettos.* New York: NCDH, 1967.

Neustadt, Richard. "The Presidency and Legislation: The Growth of Central Clearance," *American Political Science Review,* XLVIII (1954), 641–671.

———. "The Presidency and Legislation: Planning the President's Program," *American Political Science Review,* XLIX (1955), 980–1018.

Norton, Bruce. "The Committee on Banking and Currency as a Legislative Subsystem of the House of Representatives." First draft of doctoral dissertation, Syracuse University, 1968.

Olson, Mancur. *The Logic of Collective Action.* Cambridge, Mass.:

Harvard University Press, 1965.

Polsby, Nelson. *Community Power and Political Theory*. New Haven, Conn.: Yale University Press, 1963.

Presthus, Robert. *Men at the Top*. New York: Oxford University Press, 1964.

Ranney, Austin, ed. *Political Science and Public Policy*. Chicago: Markham Publishing Co., 1968.

"Redistricted Rent Supplements Funded by Bare Margin," *Congressional Quarterly Almanac*, 1966, pp. 245–249.

"Republican Housing Bill Introduced in Both Chambers," *Congressional Quarterly*, April 28, 1967, p. 687.

Salisbury, Robert. "The Analysis of Public Policy: A Search for Theories and Roles." Unpublished manuscript.

Schattschneider, E. D. *The Semi-Sovereign People*. New York: Holt, Rinehart and Winston, 1960.

Schorr, Alvin. *Slums and Social Insecurity*. Washington, D.C.: U.S. Government Printing Office, 1963.

Semple, Robert. "Signing of the Model Cities Bill Ends a Long Struggle to Keep it Alive," New York *Times*, November 4, 1966, p. 1.

Siegelman, Leonore R. "A Technical Note on Housing Census Comparability, 1950–60," *Journal of the American Institute of Planners*, XXIX (February, 1963), 51–52.

Simon, Herbert. "Notes on the Observation and Measurement of Political Power," *Introductory Readings in Political Behavior*, ed. S. Sidney Ullmer, pp. 363–376. Chicago: Rand McNally, 1961.

Stanley, David T., Dean E. Mann, and Jameson W. Doig. *Men Who Govern*. Washington, D.C.: The Brookings Institution, 1967.

Steiner, Gilbert. *Social Insecurity: The Politics of Welfare*. Chicago: Rand McNally, 1966.

Sternlieb, George. *The Tenement Landlord*. New Brunswick, N.H.: The William Byrd Press, Inc., 1966.

Truman, David. *The Governmental Process*. New York: Alfred A. Knopf, 1951.

U.S. Congress, Senate Subcommittee on Executive Reorganization of the Committee on Government Operations, *Hearings, Federal Role in Urban Affairs*, 89th Cong., 2nd Sess., 1966; 90th Cong., 1st Sess., 1967.

U.S. Congress, Senate Committee on Finance, *Hearings on S. 2100, Tax Incentives to Encourage Housing in Urban Poverty Areas*, 90th Cong., 1st Sess., 1967.

U.S. Congress, Senate Subcommittee on Housing, Committee on Banking and Currency, *Hearings, Housing Legislation of 1965*, 89th Cong., 1st Sess., 1965.

U.S. Congress, Senate Subcommittee on Housing and Urban Affairs, Committee on Banking and Currency, *Hearings on Housing Legislation of 1967*, 90th Cong., 1st Sess., 1967.

U.S. Department of Commerce, Bureau of the Census. *United States Census of Population, 1960, United States Summary, Number of Inhabitants*. Washington, D. C.: United States Government Printing Office, 1961.

Walton, John. "The Current State of Research on Community Power," *American Journal of Sociology*, LXXI (Jan., 1966), 430–438.

Warner, Lloyd W., Paul P. Van Riper, Norman H. Martin, and Orvis F. Collins. *The American Federal Executive*. New Haven, Conn.: Yale University Press, 1963.

Weaver, Robert. *The Urban Complex*. New York: Doubleday, 1960.

Wildavsky, Aaron. *The Politics of the Budgetary Process*. Boston: Little, Brown, 1964.

Wilson, James Q., ed. *Urban Renewal: The Record and the Controversy*. Cambridge, Mass.: MIT Press, 1966.

Wolman, Harold. "Towards an Understanding of Poverty." Unpublished manuscript.

# APPENDIX 1

## Methodology

As might be expected of a study so closely related to the community power studies, the most difficult methodological question was how to identify the decision-makers. The method by which the elite is identified in studies dealing with decision-making elites has been a subject of quite heated debate. There are three possible approaches to elite-identification, each one with its own advantages and disadvantages. The easiest, but least acceptable, is the positional method. The influentials are deemed to be those who hold the formal positions of authority in the political system under study. Obviously, however, this begs the questions: Who *are* the most influential? and Does influence coincide with formal position? These are empirical questions, not definitional ones, as the positional technique would suggest.

The approach which has appealed to most sociologists is the reputational method. In brief, the basis of this approach consists of setting up a panel of knowledgeable people and asking each of them to rank in order a specific number of men whom they believe to have the most influence in the area under consideration. The results are then brought together and a single list of influentials is compiled. The major advantage to this method is again simplicity; unlike the positional approach, however, the naming of influentials is a result of an investigation, not of employing definition. The major disadvantage cited is that it is not actual behavior but reputation which is being studied according to this method and there is no *a priori* reason to believe the two coincide.

The archetype of the reputational approach is often considered to be Floyd Hunter's *Community Power Structure* (1953). This is somewhat unfortunate, for Hunter's approach encompasses several difficulties which are not necessarily endemic to the reputational method. First, Hunter asks his panel to name the ten most influential people—without specifying influential in what respect. Thus, as Polsby points out, this ignores the possibility that people influential in one important issue area (e.g., education) may not be the same people influential in another (e.g., housing). Nelson Polsby suggests that each issue area ought to be studied independently and if any overlap of influentials between different areas does exist, it will be easily ascertained.[1] However, Polsby's criticism here is one of the ways in which Hunter has used the reputational method, not of the method itself. Influentials *could* have been compiled for single-issue areas by the reputational method.

Another criticism of Hunter concerns the selection of his panel, which consisted of a relatively small number of people, apparently all business executives and professional people.[2] The influentials themselves were then faced with the list of forty influentials and asked to choose the ten top leaders. The question asked was: "If a project were before the community that required decision by a group of leaders—leaders that nearly everyone would accept— which 10 on the list of 40 would you choose?" [3]

It is immediately obvious that this question does not address itself to the problem of who are (or even have the reputation of being) the most influential. Instead, it asks: Which group of ten leaders would you want to decide a community problem, providing that those ten leaders have to be generally acceptable to all others? This, of course, excludes the possibility of any conflict showing up in the elite structure and ensures a finding of a monolithic decision-making structure. Again, however, what is at fault is Hunter's application—not the reputational technique itself. It is

[1] Nelson W. Polsby, *Community Power and Political Theory* (New Haven, Conn.: Yale University Press, 1963), Chap. 6.

[2] Floyd Hunter, *Community Power Structure* (Chapel Hill: University of North Carolina Press, 1953), Appendix. Hunter's description of his methodology is extremely sketchy.

[3] *Ibid.*, p. 63.

possible to select a representative panel and to ask them a question directly concerned with influence—though such a question is exceedingly difficult to word so that it means the same thing to everyone.

The approach to elite-identification recommended by most political scientists, however, is known as the decisional method. The way to determine influentials, this method specifies, is to study the actual behavior of men involved in several decisions in the same functional area. Since several issues are studied, generalizations can be made concerning power and influence which factor out idiosyncratic variables that might show up as highly important if a traditional single case study were the sole determinant. What the decisional analysts (Polsby calls them "pluralist researchers") recommend instead is several case studies. The advantages of this approach seem significant, particularly when compared to the obvious disadvantages to alternative approaches. Actual behavior rather than reputation or position, is the variable under study, it is claimed. But the corresponding disadvantage is the large amount of resources and effort necessary to expend on this approach, particularly time and manpower.

The claim that the decisional approach involves direct study of actual behavior, while other methods involve only study of reputation, deserves close scrutiny; for this is not nearly as self-evident as its adherents state it is. What *is* actual behavior and how can it be studied directly? Behavior can be considered to consist of physical acts; to study it directly means to observe it directly. But, indeed, do those who use the decisional method directly observe behavior? The fact is, they do so very rarely. Many important decisions are made in circumstances closed or partially closed to political scientists. Further, all decisions studied which have occurred prior to the study cannot be directly observed either. It seems clear that those who engage in decisional studies do not study actual behavior directly; rather they reconstruct as best they can from secondhand reports by others, from written documents, and from interviews after the fact with participants.

In point of fact, however, how much does this differ from the reputational adherents who compile lists of individuals whom other supposedly informed individuals deem influential? By the decisional method, the political scientist himself compiles a list of influentials deemed influential, but much of the data from that list comes from the descriptions of others concerning who are influentials in making decisions. Certainly, the decisional approach is more flexible, and in that respect, undoubtedly superior. But it may be little different in kind from the reputational method, particularly a reputational method in which great care is taken to select the panel.

This study, for a variety of reasons, was undertaken with the intention of utilizing the reputational approach. The most compelling reason was the type of power structure under study. Only redistributive decisions, that is decisions perceived to involve significant social change, were under consideration. At the time the study was undertaken, only one such decision had occurred since the birth of HUD—the Model Cities Legislation.[4] For reasons already discussed, a case study of one decision was not sufficient to satisfy the theoretical aims of the study. To go back any further in time before HUD's formation might have built a bias into the study, for a fairly significant turnover in personnel occurred when HHFA became a Department. The pre-HUD housing decision-making system was thus not the same as the post-HUD system, or rather, it could not be assumed that the two systems were the same. A comparison between the two might, indeed, have been intriguing, but that was not the purpose of the study.

What was desired was a list of individuals who, during the years 1965–68, had had (and in the present were continuing to have) a major influence on redistributive decisions. The reputational method was originally determined to be quite adequate for that task, providing care was taken to select a good panel and provid-

[4] During the course of the study, redistributive policy decisions occurred which reoriented both FHA and urban renewal programs.

ing the selected panel was asked a carefully worded question which would elicit the desired response. Unfortunately, neither of these conditions was easy to satisfy, and the second, in particular, posed such a problem that, in light of previous attempts to cope with it, doubt was cast over the work of almost all previous studies done by the reputational technique.

The best panel would undoubtedly have consisted of people who were, themselves, likely to be influentials and who would, therefore, from their experience, be able to provide the most accurate recounting of who the other influential participants were. Unfortunately, since the study design called for interviewing the influentials once they were identified, it was decided that possible influentials must be excluded from the panel rather than included. The basis of this decision may have been prosaic, but it was real nonetheless. Most of the influentials were busy and important people (Congressmen, high level bureaucrats, etc.) and it was feared that they would not readily submit to two separate interviews. Therefore, care was taken to select panel members who were active participants and close observers, but who would not be likely to turn up on the list of influentials itself. Inevitably, a few of the panelists did, in the end, make the list of influentials. In order to compensate for having to work with a "second-best" panel, a correspondingly large number of panelists was interviewed—about forty altogether. Care was taken to select panelists from various perspectives so that all points in the policy process might be illuminated.

However, it was the interview itself that provided the biggest problem. At the beginning of the interview, the panelists were told, after they were guaranteed anonymity:

I am interested in finding out who the most influential people are in the making of national policy dealing with the housing of low-income people. The question I would like you to answer is: If there were to be a major policy proposal this year in the area of housing for low-income people (and I realize there is not), who would be the most influential people in bringing about or stopping the bringing about of this change? Could you please rank them in order of importance?

Note that scope was carefully specified (housing for low-income people), to avoid one of the most common criticisms of Hunter's technique. Note also that the question allows for specification of opposition, so that redistributive changes which were defeated could also be considered, thereby avoiding another pitfall. In addition, after responses were made to this question, the panelist was handed a list of nearly 150 names of possible influentials and asked whether any of those should join the list he had already volunteered.

This rather elaborate procedure (which does not differ greatly from many other reputational studies) proved a complete failure during the pretest. The main problem was that people were influential in different stages of the decision-making process and it was impossible to compare influence of people who did not interact on a similar plane. The analogy would have been the old one of comparing apples and oranges.

Thus, a new model of the decision-making process had to be developed to displace the faulty original model, a model which has been implicit in many though not all of the power studies. This implicit model had viewed decision-making as a process which took place at a single specified time around a table at which were seated all the participants in the process. The new model specified distinct stages in the process and distinct types of influence. After initial study, six stages were settled upon as providing a useful model. Panelists were then asked to name the most influential persons in each of these six stages (they were not asked to rank the persons, as this proved not only time-consuming and difficult, but also useless, given the lack of a common criterion on which to base the rankings). The six stages, and the questions asked the panelists about each were: [5]

*Idea Stage*—Who would likely be the originators of the proposals and the ideas which would most likely be accepted and ultimately enacted into law?

[5] These questions were preceded by the general introductory statement quoted, p. 199.

*Administrative Adoption Stage*—If the Administration were to adopt an idea or a proposal as its own, who would be the people who must be convinced and who would be the most influential at convincing them, either to adopt or not adopt the proposal?

*Pre-Congressional Committee Stage*—Who would be the most influential people in terms of taking a proposal the administration is considering or has accepted and modifying it or shaping it significantly (or preventing such modification or shaping) before it is presented for Congressional committee consideration?

*Legislative Passage Stage*—Who would be the most influential people in determining the nature of changes made in a proposal once it was introduced in Congress, and, indeed, in determining whether such a proposal passes or fails?

*Appropriations Stage*—Who would be the most influential people in determining budgetary levels and appropriations for new housing programs for low-income people?

*Operations Stage*—Who would be the most influential people in determining the criteria for any important guidelines on which grants are made and programs carried out? [6]

A listing of the stages suggests the difficulty encountered in not using them. How does one compare the influence of someone on a task force who sets forth the broad outlines of a major new proposal, to that of a member of the Appropriations Committee who may be the key man in determining how much funding the final form of the proposal will receive? The two individuals may never interact, thus even though the activities of both are obviously of critical importance as far as final policy output is concerned, how can they be compared with respect to influence? Policy output consists of a series of decisions, and, in effect, these two individuals would be involved in different decisions.

The procedure finally used emphasized as much flexibility as possible. Panelists were not necessarily asked to name influentials

---

[6] It should be understood that these six stages do not always occur in the exact order listed (indeed, some occur simultaneously), nor even that all six stages are invariably present. Indeed, at times different stages may collapse so that two or more are indistinguishable from one another. I am not positing a theory of the decision-making process, but rather a conceptual framework which will prove useful in determining the decision-making structure.

in all six stages, but only in those stages with which there was reason to believe they were well acquainted. Not only were they asked to name influentials, but also they were asked to explain why they named those whom they did and, if possible, to buttress their explanations with examples. As the interviews proceeded, this procedure was shortened so that panelists were asked to discuss only those named who, on the basis of previous interviews, had not already definitely been designated as influentials. The final selection of influentials was not made by any mechanical method. Rather, it was made on the basis of the author's own judgment, taking into account not only frequency of designation as an influential, but also reliability of the panelists who mentioned them (some panelists were judged to be more informed than others), and the quality of the explanations and the examples given. Thus, an individual mentioned only two or three times, but each time by a panelist who had himself participated in important decisions in which the individual in question had been influential, would likely end up an influential; whereas someone mentioned much more frequently, but by panelists who themselves were further from the policy process and who could provide no convincing examples, might be left off the list.

In addition, the interviews with the panelists were viewed as opportune times to garner information about the conversion process. These wide-ranging and unstructured interviews form the basis of Chapters 4–7.

### Interviewing the Elite

The interviews with the influentials themselves presented several problems. It appeared that a structured interview schedule was called for, but the best form for the questions was not at all obvious. Open-ended questions with much probing would have provided more information in depth—but they would have taken much longer. Since the interviewees were very busy people, it was decided that an hour would be the maximum limit for one interview. Thus, open-ended questions would have meant diminishing the scope of the study. Certainly, this would have been a feasible alternative, but one the author chose to ignore in order to pursue the broader theoretical interests of the study.

As a result, closed-ended questions were decided upon with the realization that as complete an ordering of alternatives as possible had to be provided. Unfortunately, the pre-tests demonstrated that a complete listing of alternatives was not possible. More important, some respondents showed a strong antipathy to some of the closed questions—a factor which greatly inhibited rapport and, indeed, threw some doubt on the validity of their response.

As a result, it was decided to make as many questions as possible open-ended, consistent with the time restraints. The questions about role perception were closed because the pre-tests showed that the alternatives presented opened up legitimate alternatives to the respondent that he would not have considered under an open-ended question.

It must be admitted that the pre-tests themselves were not entirely satisfactory. They were performed on a number of people who had substantial knowledge of housing policy, but these people were not at all representative of the elite population to be interviewed. Indeed, it was impossible to pre-test on any of the elite since the entire membership, and not simply a sample of it, was ultimately to be interviewed. The only way to deal with this problem was to make several adjustments in the interview schedule after five or six interviews had been completed when it became obvious that some questions which had pre-tested well on the nonelite were ineffective on the elite itself.

Obtaining appointments for interviews was not difficult in the bureaucracy and in lobby or professional groups, but presented major problems where elected politicians were concerned.[7] As a result, in fourteen cases, second best had to be settled for, and an as-

---

[7] Congress, in particular, has been overstudied by political scientists to the point where Congressmen are wary when one approaches them. The one-way nature of social science interviews has perhaps not been sufficiently appreciated. Politicians have extremely full schedules and there is very little to gain (and possibly a good deal to lose if confidence is violated) by granting an interview to an academic.

sistant of the influential was called into service to respond for the influential. Wherever possible, that assistant was the individual who handled housing affairs for the elected official, and, thus, in most cases was indeed the influential, so far as housing was concerned. This conception views a Congressman or a mayor as an institution, not simply as an individual.

In two cases, it was necessary to forego a direct oral interview and to settle for a mail response. In such cases, the need for the influential himself to fill out the schedule was stressed, but, of course, there was no way of knowing whether, in fact, this procedure was followed. Three of the influentials categorically refused to be interviewed.

# APPENDIX 2

## Communications Patterns

Floyd Hunter's community power study of Atlanta at times seems to suggest that policy in Atlanta derived from a small group of men, all of whom were friendly with one another and who met to make major decisions as they were needed. Critics have called this the conspiracy theory of American politics. They have accused researchers such as Hunter of not specifying the scope [1] of their inquiry when they go about their research. In this study, the scope was clearly specified as low-income housing decisions and the decision-making process was subdivided into four stages: policy formulation, legislative, appropriations, and operations. Each of these stages is important in redistributive decision-making. They were

[1] See Appendix 1.

investigated separately, so that if a person was influential in more than one stage, it could be easily determined.

Of the 68 decision-makers, 35 were involved in the policy-formulation stage, 32 in the legislative stage, 20 in the appropriations stage, and only 16 in the operations stage. Table 16 lists the number of decision-makers in each stage and the total number of stages each decision-maker was in.

**Table 16.** Total Number of Stages per Each Decision-Maker

| Number in each stage | One stage | Two stages | Three stages | All stages | Total |
|---|---|---|---|---|---|
| Policy formulation | 19 | 11 | 0 | 5 | 35 |
| Legislative | 13 | 13 | 1 | 5 | 32 |
| Appropriations | 8 | 6 | 1 | 5 | 20 |
| Operations | 4 | 6 | 1 | 5 | 16 |
| TOTAL [a] | 44 | 18 | 1 | 5 | |

[a] To get the total number of decision-makers involved in two stages, it was necessary to divide the total in the second column by two because of double counting (a person influential both in the policy formulation and legislative stages was listed in both the policy formulation—two-stage cell—and the legislative —two-stage cell). Similarly the total in the three-stage column was divided by three and the four-stage column by four.

Forty-four of the decision-makers were influential only in one stage; on the other hand, five of the decision-makers were influential in all stages. The five influential in all stages were Special Assistant to the President Joseph Califano; HUD Secretary Robert Weaver; HUD Undersecretary Robert Wood; Philip Hanna of the Bureau of the Budget Housing Division; and John Gunther, Executive Director of the Conference of Mayors. Although these five are major influentials, taken together they hardly constitute evidence of a conspiracy which can determine the nature of the country's housing policy. They are active and influential in each stage because of the nature of the positions they hold, *but* they do not and cannot dominate each stage. In short, although they are perhaps the most active influentials, there is no reason to believe they are the most powerful. Senator John Sparkman, who is influential in only one stage—the substantive legislative stage—is surely more powerful in that stage than any of the five, as is Representative George Mahon in the appropriations stage. There seems to be relatively little overlap of influentials between various stages of the policy process.

# APPENDIX 3

## *List of Influentials*

### *CONGRESSMEN*

SEN. GORDON ALLOT (R—Col.), Ranking Minority Member, Independent Offices Subcommittee Senate Appropriations

REP. THOMAS ASHLEY (D—O.), Housing Subcommittee, House Banking and Currency Committee

SEN. ALLEN ELLENDER (D—La.), Independent Offices Subcommittee, Senate Appropriations Committee

REP. JOE EVINS (D—Tenn.), *Chairman*, Independent Offices Subcommittee, House Appropriations Committee

REP. JAMES HARVEY (R—Mich.), Former Member, Housing Subcommittee, House Banking and Currency Committee

REP. CHARLES JONAS (R—N.C.), Ranking Minority Member, Independent Offices Subcommittee, House Appropriations Committee

SEN. ROBERT KENNEDY (D—N.Y.)

SEN. WARREN MAGNUSON (D—Wash.), *Chairman*, Subcommittee on Urban Affairs, Senate Appropriations Committee

REP. GEORGE MAHON (D—Tex.), *Chairman*, House Appropriations Committee

SEN. WALTER MONDALE (D—Minn.), Housing Subcommittee, Senate Banking and Currency Committee

SEN. EDMUND MUSKIE (D–Me.), Housing Subcommittee, Senate Banking and Currency Committee

SEN. JOHN PASTORE (D–R.I.), Independent Offices Subcommittee, Senate Appropriations Committee

REP. WRIGHT PATMAN (D–Tex.), *Chairman*, House Banking and Currency Committee

SEN. CHARLES PERCY (R–Ill.), Housing Subcommittee, Senate Banking and Currency Committee

SEN. ABRAHAM RIBICOFF (D–Conn.), *Chairman*, Subcommittee on Executive Reorganization, Government Operations Committee

SEN. JOHN SPARKMAN (D–Ala.), *Chairman* of both Subcommittee on Housing and Full Committee, Senate Banking and Currency Committee

REP. ROBERT STEPHENS (D–Ga.), Housing Subcommittee, House Banking and Currency Committee

REP. LEONOR SULLIVAN (D–Mo.), Subcommittee on Housing, House Banking and Currency Committee

REP. WILLIAM WIDNALL (R–N.J.), Ranking Minority Member, Housing Subcommittee, House Banking and Currency Committee

## CONGRESSIONAL ASSISTANTS

JOHN BARRIERE, Former Director Housing Subcommittee, House Banking and Currency, presently attached to staff of Speaker McCormack

CARL COAN, SR., Staff Director, Housing Subcommittee, Senate Banking and Currency Committee

HARLEY DIRKS, Staff Director, Independent Offices Subcommittee, Senate Appropriations Committee

CASEY IRELAND, Minority Staff Director, Housing Subcommittee, House Banking and Currency Committee

JON MACGUIRE, Assistant to Sen. Walter Mondale

JAMES MCEWEN, Staff Director, Housing Subcommittee, House Banking and Currency Committee

DONALD NICOLL, Assistant to Sen. Edmund Muskie

## HUD OFFICIALS

PHILIP BROWNSTEIN, Assistant Secretary for Mortgage Credit and Federal Housing Commissioner

JOSEPH BURSTEIN, formerly General Counsel, Public Housing Administration, currently in General Counsel's Office, Office of the Secretary

ASHLEY FOARD, General Counsel's Office, Office of the Secretary

JOHN FRANTZ, Director, Office of Budget

CHARLES HAAR, Assistant Secretary for Metropolitan Development
JAY JANIS, Executive Assistant to the Secretary
EDWARD LASHMAN, Assistant to the Secretary for Congressional Services
CARTER MCFARLAND, Assistant Commissioner, Federal Housing Administration
ROBERT MC CABE, Deputy Assistant Secretary for Renewal Assistance
WILLIAM ROSS, Deputy Undersecretary
HENRY SCHECHTER, Director, Office of Economics and Market Analysis
RALPH TAYLOR, Assistant Secretary for Demonstrations and Intergovernmental Relations (Model Cities)
ROBERT WEAVER, Secretary
ROBERT WOOD, Undersecretary

*EXECUTIVE OFFICE OF
THE PRESIDENT AND OTHER GOVERNMENT OFFICIALS*
FRED BOHEN, Assistant to the President
JOSEPH CALIFANO, Special Assistant to the President
WILLIAM CAREY, Assistant Director, Bureau of the Budget
JAMES DUESENBERRY, Member, Council of Economic Advisers
PHILIP HANNA, Assistant Director, Housing and Urban Development, Human Resources Program Division, Bureau of the Budget
SHERMAN MAISEL, Governor, Federal Reserve Board
HOWARD MOSCOF, Staff Director, Kaiser Committee
CHARLES SCHULTZE, Director, Bureau of the Budget

*MAYORS*
MAYOR JEROME CAVANAGH, Detroit
MAYOR RICHARD DALEY, Chicago
MAYOR JOHN LINDSAY, New York

*OTHERS*
ANDREW BIEMILLER, Director, Legislative Department, AFL-CIO
LARRY BLACKMON, Past President, National Association of Home Builders
JACK CONWAY, Executive Director, Industrial Union Division, AFL-CIO
JOHN GUNTHER, Executive Director, U.S. Conference of Mayors
PAT HEALY, Executive Director, National League of Cities
BEN HEINEMAN, Chairman, Chicago & Northwestern Railroad
EDGAR KAISER, Chairman, Kaiser Committee (President's Commission on Urban Housing)
JOSEPH KEENAN, International Secretary of the Brotherhood of Electrical Workers, member of Kaiser Committee

SAUL KLAMAN, Executive Vice-President, National Association of Mutual Savings Banks

DAVID KROOTH, Chairman of Legislative Committee and Resolutions Committee, National Housing Conference

RAYMOND NASHER, President, Nasher Industries, member of Kaiser Committee

WILLIAM RAFSKY, President, National Association of Housing and Redevelopment Officials

WILLIAM SLAYTON, Former Commissioner of Urban Renewal, presently Executive Vice-President, Urban America

LEON WEINER, President, National Association of Home Builders, member of Kaiser Committee

WILLIAM WHEATON, Professor, University of California (Berkeley)

PAUL YLVISAKER, Community Relations Director, New Jersey Department of Community Affairs

WHITNEY YOUNG, Executive Director, Urban League

# APPENDIX 4

*Low-Rent Public Housing under Public Law 171 as Amended*

| Year | Active Housing Units | |
|---|---|---|
| | *Constructed or obtained— annual contributions contracts executed* | *Completed or obtained— acquired with or without rehabilitation, or leased* [a] |
| 1949 | 0 | 0 |
| 1950 | 78,248 | 270 |
| 1951 | 88,929 | 9,994 |
| 1952 | 41,513 | 58,258 |
| 1953 | 10,406 | 58,384 |
| 1954 | 0 | 44,293 |

## APPENDIX 4 (continued)

*Low-Rent Public Housing under Public Law 171 as Amended*

| | Active Housing Units | |
|---|---|---|
| Year | Constructed or obtained— annual contributions contracts executed | Completed or obtained— acquired with or without rehabilitation, or leased [a] |
| 1955 | 29,965 | 20,899 |
| 1956 | 43,097 | 11,993 |
| 1957 | 5,391 | 10,513 |
| 1958 | 24,293 | 15,472 |
| 1959 | 29,770 | 21,939 |
| 1960 | 11,437 | 16,401 |
| 1961 | 27,867 | 20,965 |
| 1962 | 25,094 | 28,682 |
| 1963 | 36,031 | 27,327 |
| 1964 | 37,429 | 24,488 |
| 1965 | 26,281 | 30,769 |
| 1966 | 43,514 | 31,483 |
| 1967 | 70,283 | 39,011 |
| 1968 | 79,693 | 71,695 |

[a] Includes all completed units, some of which have been removed from dwelling use.

SOURCE: Housing Assistance Administration.

## APPENDIX 5

*Housing Units in Federal Low-Rent Public Housing Programs*

| Year and Type | Cumulated from September 1, 1937<br>As of July 1969 |
|---|---|
| Low-rent public housing<br>annual contributions<br>contracts executed | |
| Total | |
| 1967 | 837,473 |
| 1968 | 875,551 |
| 1969 | 989,763 |
| In preconstruction | |
| 1967 | 135,221 |
| 1968 | 112,518 |
| 1969 | 128,784 |
| Under construction | |
| 1967 | 44,835 |
| 1968 | 53,817 |
| 1969 | 69,151 |
| Under management,<br>Total | |
| 1967 | 657,417 |
| 1968 | 709,216 |
| 1969 | 791,828 |
| Turnkey, new | |
| 1967 | 371 |
| 1968 | 2,829 |
| 1969 | 16,174 |
| Leased | |
| 1967 | 5,247 |
| 1968 | 21,870 |
| 1969 | 45,819 |

## APPENDIX 5 (continued)

*Housing Units in Federal Low-Rent Public Housing Programs*

| | *Cumulated from September 1, 1937* |
|---|---|
| *Year and Type* | *As of July 1969* |
| Conventional, new | |
| 1967 | 644,501 |
| 1968 | 671,303 |
| 1969 | 705,618 |
| Acquisition[a] | |
| 1967 | 7,298 |
| 1968 | 13,214 |
| 1969 | 24,217 |

[a] Includes units with rehabilitation and without rehabilitation.
SOURCE: Housing Assistance Administration.

## APPENDIX 6

# Abbreviations: Federal Agencies, Government Terms and Programs, Organizations Interested in Housing

ABA (American Bankers Association)
AFDC (Aid to Families with Dependent Children)
AFSC (American Friends Service Committee)
AIP (American Institute of Planners)
BOB (Bureau of the Budget)
BRC (Budget Review Committee)

CAP (Community Action Program)
CEA (Council of Economic Advisers)
CORE (Congress of Racial Equality)
FHA (Federal Housing Administration)
FNMA (Federal National Mortgage Association)
GNMA (Government National Mortgage Association)
HEW (Health, Education, and Welfare)
HHFA (Housing and Home Finance Agency)
HUD (Department of Housing and Urban Development)
MBA (Mortgage Bankers Association)
NAACP (National Association for the Advancement of Colored People)
NAHB (National Association of Home Builders)
NAHRO (National Association of Housing and Redevelopment Officials)
NAREB (National Association of Real Estate Boards)
NCDH (National Committee against Discrimination in Housing)
NHC (National Housing Conference)
NLC (National League of Cities)
OEO (Office of Economic Opportunity)
OLR (Office of Legislative Reference, Bureau of the Budget)
PAC (Project Area Committees)
PHA (Public Housing Administration)
PPBS (Program-Planning Budget System)
PWA (Public Works Administration)
SMSA (Standard Metropolitan Statistical Area)
SNCC (Student Non-Violent Coordinating Committee)
USS & LA (U.S. Savings and Loan Association)
USHA (United States Housing Authority)
VA (Veterans Administration)

# Index

## Date Due

| | | | |
|---|---|---|---|
| | | | |
| | | | |
| | | | |
| | | | |
| | | | |
| | | DEC-20 | |
| | | | |
| | | | |
| | | | |
| | | | |
| | | | |
| | | | |
| | | | |
| | | | |
| | | | |